PARTNERS IN PLAY

Partners in Play

A STEP-BY-STEP GUIDE
TO IMAGINATIVE PLAY IN CHILDREN

Dorothy G. Singer and Jerome L. Singer

Drawings by Sandy Rabinowitz

HARPER & ROW, PUBLISHERS

New York, Hagerstown, San Francisco, London

1817

FIRST EDITION

Designed by Sidney Feinberg

Library of Congress Cataloging in Publication Data

Singer, Dorothy G
    Partners in play.
    Bibliography: p.
    Includes index.
    1. Play. 2. Imagination in children.
3. Creative activities and seat work. I. Singer,
Jerome L., joint author. II. Title.
BF717.S515   1977   155.4'18   75–30346
ISBN 0–06–013891–2

77 78 79 80 1 2 3 4 5 6 7 8 9 10

*This book is for Jon, Bruce
and Jeff*

Contents

Preface

The human imagination is still one of the great untapped resources for the development of the growing child's ability to learn, to evolve a sense of self, and simply to enjoy the pleasures of his or her own creative capacities. While almost all preschool children show a natural growth of imaginative skills, they need the encouragement and leadership of parents and nursery school and kindergarten teachers to sustain and broaden the scope of their constructive play. This book has grown out of extensive research by ourselves and others and our own direct involvement with preschoolers. We have explored a range of exercises and games designed to help preschool children expand their imaginative horizons and enjoy their own play more. The procedures, suggestions, exercises and games presented in this book will help parents and teachers play more effectively with children, and will foster the *independent* development of imaginative resources as well.

Our format consists of brief general discussions of the importance of different aspects of make-believe play and imagination in healthy growth, followed by a series of specific exercises or games suitable for use at home or in the day care center, nursery school or kindergarten. We have tested these exercises and suggestions with a wide variety of children from two through five, and they have also been used by other workers. They are based on the best scientific evidence, are simple and practical, and are also such fun that parents and teachers will find the time they spend with young children much more enjoyable.

For parents interested in books, records, music and toys that can heighten the child's imagination, we have included an extensive list of materials appropriate for children aged two through five. A scientific reference list is provided for readers who would like to explore the psychological research literature on make-believe and sociodramatic play. The main thesis of this book, however, is that fantasy and creativity can be stimulated with a minimum of props. The *enthusiasm* of a concerned and knowledgeable adult, who uses some of the games, stories and exercises we describe, is the best of tools for arousing the child's imaginative resources.

Our own close associations with Joan Freyberg, who carried out an important early experiment in this field, and with Roni Tower, who worked closely with us in developing some of the materials lists and theoretical references, were personally rewarding. The editorial advice of Ann Harris and Maria Guarnaschelli and the clerical assistance of Esta Schaffer and Judith McBride are gratefully acknowledged. This book is dedicated to our sons Jon, Bruce and Jeff, who afforded us the personal pleasure of being their partners in play through many exciting years. We wish, finally, to acknowledge the many children whom we have watched and played with in nursery schools such as Elmwood in White Plains, New York; Pinafore in Shelton, Connecticut; the Yale University Child Study Center; the Mother Goose Nursery in Woodbridge, Connecticut; and the Bridgeport (Connecticut) Jewish Center Nursery School.

PARTNERS IN PLAY

Introduction: What Make-Believe Can Do for Children

Let us take a look at some four-year-old boys and girls at play in a nursery school. Some of them are climbing on the indoor Junglegym, trying to get across as fast as they possibly can, then demonstrating their strength by swinging higher and higher before jumping down to the ground. Others are piling one block on top of another to see how high a tower they can build before it falls. Clearly a good deal of the play that goes on involves the children's developing a simple physical *mastery* of the environment, testing their own coordination and strength. Often, however, the swingers may be pretending they are sea adventurers of old, climbing into an old fortress to rescue an imprisoned member of their band. The block-pilers may pretend the towers are skyscrapers being shaken by earthquakes, or organize their blocks into "cities" or "space stations." The children are using the blocks or swings to represent objects or situations quite different from what they actually are. Some children grouped around the small sandbox are pretending it contains an island, to which a little pipe cleaner boat floating on make-believe water is traveling back and forth. Amid much "splashing," a child shouts, "Hurricane! Danger!" and tries to move the boat safely away from the flying sand.

Making believe and pretending are among the wonders of the experience of being human. Young animals also seem to engage in various types of play, of course; they carry out a good deal of rough-and-tumble and in the case of chimpanzees or fairly advanced monkeys, occasionally even appear to pretend to threaten and to mollify each other. Chimpanzees make a kind of "play face" as if to indicate that their pushing and shoving are not to be taken as attacks; by this means they avoid getting into dangerous fights. But animal play has none of the complex pretending that involves the caretaking, the make-believe teaching and doctoring, the high adventure of exploration, crisis and conflict that delight us when we watch and listen to the play of human four- and five-year-olds. The play of animals is very close to what animals do all the time: grooming, fighting for territory, feeding. Their play never includes behavior that can be categorized as imaginative. Though children's play may anticipate some actions of adults, it includes many other *possibilities* as well, a vast array of potential or even impossible behaviors that even at this early age hint at the limitless range of the human imagination.

The Importance of Make-Believe

The four-year-olds we have just described can certainly tell the difference between a pipe cleaner and a boat. What they are doing is using whatever implements are available, some more realistic in appearance than others, and filling in the rest of the details by utilizing their own capacities for imagery. They constantly change the time and space relationships in situations, and project images into the future. Of course, a four-year-old may not stick with the story line very long. He or she may get some of the details mixed up or terminate the game abruptly and move on to another activity.

The process we observe in the child who transforms geometric blocks into a "space station" is not greatly different in its potential from that of the film director reading a script. From the bare words on a page the director envisions an elaborate complex of physical settings and human interactions, which he will actually translate through the camera into a form that others can share. The child begins with blocks and twigs and spoons, and drawing on the memories he has been storing from infancy, he too tries to develop a setting, a series of characters and a rudimentary plot.

The research of Dr. Greta Fein at Yale University has demonstrated that by eighteen months of age children already show signs of make-believe in their play, "feeding" themselves with empty spoons or cups and saying "Yummy!" The child's tendency to play and replay past events or to anticipate future ones through imagery seems to be a basic capacity of the brain that can be sustained and enlarged by the encouragement of adults.

Our human capacity to plan ahead, whether for moments, days or years, is built to a certain extent around our playful daydreams of possible events in the future and our role in them. The great neurologist Dr. Kurt Goldstein proposed that the highest human function is our ability "to take an attitude toward the possible." It requires but a moment of reflection (an example in itself of our point) for us to realize how many different ways we use our developed capacity for make-believe or fantasy as a means for anticipating practical consequences. We may play out in our mind's eye certain financial transactions we hope to undertake. We may picture how we ought to behave in certain social situations that are upcoming. Sometimes we try to experience the emotions of an important person in our lives through "picturing" that individual in different situations and attempting to feel in ourselves what he or she may be feeling. This is what psychologists call *empathy,* a critical feature of love and intimacy, and of mature concern for others. We have increasing evidence that make-believe play is preparation for the adult ability to plan ahead and to anticipate practical consequences. A childhood rich in fantasy play also lays the foundation for an adult life with well-developed imaginative and playful capacities, and with adaptive skills useful and necessary in dealing with a complex society. We are in fact suggesting that pretending and making believe, activities that start so early in childhood and continue into adult life, are basic characteristics of a rounded, fulfilled human being.

Some Specific Benefits of Make-Believe for Children

Imaginative play can make for a happy childhood, a benefit that is worthwhile in itself. Make-believe games also have specific advantages for the child, advantages which are corroborated by scientific research. We hope to demonstrate to parents and teachers how to foster and stimulate this play so that children can derive some of these major benefits.

HAPPIER CHILDREN: Our research studies indicate that children engaged in make-believe games of various kinds are more likely to be smiling, and to be giving other indications of elation, happiness and contentment. Children with less capacity for spontaneous make-believe are more likely to appear either sluggish or sad, or to become aggressive and assaultive. They disrupt the play of others, find themselves the object of their parents' or teachers' anger, and are often labeled "bad" at an early age.

SELF-AWARENESS: Children who pretend to feed themselves with an empty cup, or to feed mommy or a toy "horsy," are making important strides in self-development. They are identifying unreality but using it playfully; they are transforming empty to full, the toy animal to a real one or a human baby. Most of all, they are developing a sense of self and demonstrating their *control* over environmental objects. Professor Brian Sut-

ton-Smith of Teachers College, Columbia University, one of the world's leading scholars of play, calls attention to the sense of power over their movements and their bodies, as well as over the environment, that children gain from manipulating small objects and pretending with them.

IMAGERY SKILL: One of the great human resources for organizing and utilizing the complex information that confronts us in our environment is imagery—our ability to replay mentally a sensation that has already passed us by in time. This replication of a smell or taste or sound or sight that is no longer present is a key to the way we eventually develop the great storehouse of memories that are essential to learning and intellectual growth. Children's make-believe games depend heavily upon their resort to imagery—as when they pretend a fluffy piece of wool is a baby and imagine that it moves or talks or wets or smells. Imagery skills used in imaginative play may play a key role later in vocabulary growth, because words associated with pictures in the mind are remembered better than abstract terms. Thus imagery helps in word-building and reading. When it has been fostered in childhood imaginative play, it also adds a kind of richness or savor to the adult's life by sharpening the senses; through imagery we recapture the smells of favorite foods, the beauty of a particular sunset, the melody of a favorite song.

VERBAL SKILLS: As far as we can determine, young children do not think "within themselves" nearly as much as adults. Much of what we view as thought or the stream of consciousness is expressed directly by preschool children in words, phrases, movements or sound effects. In the course of pretending, therefore, the child blurts out everything he is experiencing or knows. When we observe children in spontaneous play, we record their sounds, bits of phrases, shouts—all uttered with changes of voice for different characters or amusing imitations of adult expressions. By *hearing* their own words or those of their playmates, children are in effect practicing vocabulary, learning new ways to express themselves and picking up phrases or nuances of the language.

DEVELOPING EMOTIONAL AWARENESS AND SENSITIVITY: In make-believe play the child may take the part of several characters, or change from his or her own role as a child to that of a parent, a doctor or a teacher. In doing this the child will not only mimic the phrases of the adult, but in a sense will be "trying on" the emotions and sense of concern adults show for children. Such play then becomes the basis for developing feelings of sympathy and empathy, and also helps the child later in grasping the more subtle aspects of an adult's communication.

LEARNING ROLES FOR NEW SOCIAL SITUATIONS: By shifting from "I'm the daddy" to "I'm the baby" or "I'm the teacher" or "I'm the policeman," children develop an awareness of the different figures they see about them and what their functions are. The child who plays school can find that school seems less frightening or alien. Research by Dr. Sara Smilansky with children in Israel who had not been adequately prepared for the routines or demands of school by their family experiences showed that when they were provided with opportunities to play make-believe school games and shift roles, they adjusted to school more easily later on. Even in games—such as adventure or exploration—that are less closely related to actual possibilities, the make-believe helps the child absorb material he encounters in history lessons, news broadcasts, television and books.

FLEXIBILITY IN NEW SOCIAL SITUATIONS: We tend to regard children as impulsive, self-centered or unable to deal flexibly with new situations. These behaviors emerge because youngsters have not yet had enough experience to make sense of the new setting. They also lack what we call *time perspective*—the ability (based on experience) to realize that certain events have a natural sequence and that the desired outcome will eventually emerge. They become impatient if they have to wait for the hamburger to cook or must wait their turn at the barber's or the doctor's. Pretending, talking to themselves and imaginative play help children develop self-control during such waiting situations and make them less likely to become upset or aggressive.

The delight children take in make-believe can also serve to provide them with a positive experience. Consider the youngster marking time in a drab bus terminal waiting room. The child skilled in make-believe can take his mother's umbrella and the miniature soldiers in his pocket and create an exciting adventure of travel to a far-off land or planet, encountering monsters or strange natives or physical dangers. While he remains absorbed in the game, time passes rapidly, the bus arrives and here comes grandma down the steps! The child without the resources of make-believe is likely to become increasingly whiny, move about looking for novelty, disturb other people and end up being spoken to sharply by them. Make-believe provides a set of "tools" useful in many situations, and is also a valuable means of dealing with loneliness or confinement.

CREATIVITY: Finally, a very important advantage of make-believe and pretending is the way in which they open children up to a great deal of the curiosity, novelty and originality that so enrich all human existence. Fantasy and make-believe play increase their ability to explore new contexts and to try out new situations in odd combinations. This exploration of novelty makes children sensitive to the creativity of others, as expressed in stories or movies or art. It also lays the groundwork for their own creative development. It has been shown that men and women who demonstrated creative achievements early in their lives had engaged in a good deal of fantasy as children, and often developed imaginary companions. They had also been exposed to considerable storytelling by their parents, or played pantomime games with them.

Creative living implies much more than the production of literature or art. Our lives as adults are full of opportunities to express originality and creativity in simpler ways. The mother who quiets a temporarily frightened or uncomfortable youngster not by shouts or threats but by diverting the child with little teasing games is showing a simple yet valuable form of creativity. A young adult may be trying to break into a particular field where entry is tightly controlled by company personnel directors who merely ask for résumés and file them. By playing out in his or her mind's eye a range of possible ways of attracting the attention of executives in that field, the young person may realize that a few hundred dollars' investment in an effective trade-magazine advertisement could catch the eye of dozens of people and lead to interviews and contacts. There are literally dozens of occasions in which by taking a situation that is distressing or frightening or frustrating, and twisting it imaginatively—even carrying it to an absurd fantasy—one can lighten one's mood for a moment or discover a different way of coping with the situation.

Can Make-Believe Be Dangerous to Mental Health?

Some parents may worry that make-believe will confuse their children's ability to distinguish between reality and fantasy, or encourage them to withdraw emotionally. We have very little evidence that this ever occurs. There are a few dramatic cases described in the psychiatric literature that involve children who have spent an excessive amount of time playing fantasy games or developing imaginary kingdoms. The danger, of course, is that the child may come to so enjoy the spheres he can control himself that he avoids the necessity of dealing and interacting with other children.

We must of course avoid any circumstances in which a child who learns imaginative play will find it so appealing as to discourage real encounters with other children. Fortunately, however, excessive withdrawal into fantasy is extremely rare. In fact, most research evidence on the behavior of children who eventually show serious emotional or social difficulty indicates that those most prone to later behavioral problems are children who are extremely active, are often directly aggressive or obstreperous, and show relatively *little* development of their inner lives. More imaginative children are less likely to evidence breakdown or distress.

For the parent or teacher who is concerned about how much fantasy life is too much, the answer is relatively simple. If a child has withdrawn so completely into the world of make-believe that the learning of simple skills suffers drastically, there is no companionship at all with other children, and personal habits have become sloppy, then there is obvious reason for concern. Professional help should be sought under such circumstances. But the risk of such developments is far slighter than the much greater risk to children who fail to make sufficient use of their capacity for imagination. Our clinical observations suggest that these are the youngsters who are likely to run into serious problems in society. They often show great difficulty in dealing effectively with the anxiety and the stresses that are inevitable parts of growing up.

Let us not short-change our children by becoming prisoners of terms like "loss of touch with reality" or "living in a world of fantasy." Indeed, it is often the child with too limited a range of make-believe who is likely to focus on extremely *narrow* fantasies which lead to distortion of later reality. Sociodramatic play is really a preparation for facing complex realities, and a child's imaginative anticipation of a wide variety of situations prepares him effectively for realistic responses to these realities.

Can Make-Believe Be Taught?

While the capacity for fantasy or pretending is inherent in all reasonably normal human beings, the degree to which it is used by children depends to a large extent on whether parents or other adults have fostered it. Neglect can derive from lack of encouragement or stimulation, or from concentrating too many of one's aspirations for a child on school skills like reading or arithmetic rather than on the development of his imaginative resources. Either way, the loss to the child is serious. The child deprived of such encouragement is often apathetic, sad and lacking in play resources.

We know from the lives of many notable and creative persons in the arts and sciences that they often enjoyed early contact with an adult who directed their imagination along a particular line and played a key role in their subsequent development.

Even in the simple make-believe play of nursery school children we have clear indications that an adult can be important in changing the pattern of make-believe play that the child showed initially. For example, we carried out research with a nursery school group on the effects of a television program on the children's play. The greatest increase in spontaneous make-believe play came when the children's teacher engaged in entirely make-believe games and encouraged them to try their hand at it too. The television show also led the children to increased make-believe play, but only if an adult had been sitting with them during the show, encouraged them to pay particular attention to some of the material, and when it was over, helped them try out some of the imaginative possibilities in the plot. The children who watched television without any adult intervention at all showed the least increase in make-believe. It is clear that a parent or teacher can be of tremendous value in enhancing the imaginative capacities of the children.

Even in the first year of life, face-to-face contact with a smiling, interested, *softly speaking* adult is a tremendously important experience for the child. Throughout the early years the child needs the smiles, pleasant speech and playful reactions of a familiar adult—a mother, father, aunt, teacher or baby-sitter. That smiling face helps the child develop a sense of someone else out *there,* and this encourages a sense of *self* and *others.* Quiet times of play with the young child help him feel *important* because of the attention of the adult. The child begins to try to imitate the adult's facial expressions, words, gestures, and out of this imitation he shapes the plots for his first make-believe games.

An adult can help the child develop his imagination further by playing little games. A toy teddy bear or stuffed animal can be hidden under a chair or behind a sofa and a game of hide-and-seek engaged in, which can be very exciting to a two- or three-year-old. For the three- or four-year-old, a parent can choose some of the "outside" people who so fascinate young children—policemen, auto mechanics, firemen, supermarket cashiers or television figures—and encourage the child to pretend that simple playthings represent these individuals. Some of those quiet or "idle" moments alone with a child can turn out to be extremely important learning times if there is a playful interaction between adult and child. This can be accomplished casually and with spontaneity.

Parents often tend to *overorganize* the activities of their children, setting up too many lessons or definite tasks. From two and a half on, many children now attend school for at least part of the day, and day care centers and nurseries may keep them almost too busy. We need to strike a better balance between *structuring* children's activities and giving them a chance to play on their own. For somewhat older children there are too many formal after-school programs. Instead of unscheduled games of ball, kids now confront leagues dominated by fiercely competitive parents. Recall the *Peanuts* cartoon in which Charlie Brown learns with his characteristic wistful bewilderment that even making snowmen in winter has been organized as a little league by the parents! Our intention here is to suggest ways parents and teachers can foster play skills that will make children better able to enjoy time on their own, free of adult supervision.

Some parents believe that television is a stimulant for imaginative play. It can be very useful but only under special conditions, which will be discussed in Chapter 9. Too often television becomes no more than a baby-sitter, with children plunked in front of it so that parents can go about their chores. The prepackaged fantasies of television cannot help children develop enough of their *own* skills to fill quiet time. It is very easy for children to become dependent on the outside stimulation of the tube instead of relying on their own capacities.

We believe that children are best served when they can develop a skill, initially with adult help, that they can soon exercise independently, *free of outside intervention.* When adults offer consistent encouragement of make-believe skills, children become able to move off on their own, creating lively and exciting new environments for themselves. And these skills, which our research indicates are well established in some children by four years of age, can serve throughout life as a reservoir of personal resourcefulness, liveliness, creativity and self-esteem.

The teacher or parent has a critical role in the child's development of play skills, a role that has been relatively neglected. The adult can convey to the playing child a sense of involvement and emotional warmth. Once the game or activity is started, however, the adult should step back somewhat and allow the child to pursue his own direction. What emerges is likely to be an exciting and lively interchange between them around an increasingly imaginative and complex story line. The adult contribution is critical; but having shown the child the excitement of play, he or she should know enough not to dominate the game or organize the play too highly. The reward is watching the child bloom in the spirit of the game.

In the present volume therefore, we are proposing a series of approaches to make-believe play with preschool children. These exercises and games can be carried out by parents at home with their own children, or by nursery school teachers or day care center staff members. The games and exercises are intrinsically interesting to children, encourage skills, help them learn to play with their peers, and are a source of delight to both adult and child.

Children can play with adults in many ways. In these pages we are most interested in imaginative and make-believe forms of play. Obviously, children also learn a great deal from playing checkers or athletic games with their parents, and from mastery games such as blocks and Tinker Toy structures. Frequently parents and nursery school teachers are hesitant to go on to the

next step in the course of such play, which is to accept or
encourage the make-believe elements that children add spontaneously to these games.

A note of caution to the parents or teachers who try the
exercises or games that will be set forth here. Our materials can
be employed with children between the ages of two and five.
Those three years are periods of great change and growth. The
two-year-old has a small vocabulary, limited motor coordination
and very little concept of time or space, different colors, numbers and other abstractions we take for granted in older children and adults. Don't present children with tasks or exercises
too far beyond their capacity. A little stretching of the mind is
fine—that's where children pick up the new ideas they then
attempt to assimilate in the course of symbolic play. But be alert
to the fact that for the two-year-old, notions of color or complicated story plots are merely confusing. Don't take it for granted
that children will understand commonplace phrases or have a
grasp of metaphor. A three-year-old child we know heard a
storekeeper described as "a pretty sharp fellow" and asked,
"Does that mean he bites?"

Remember also that playing with preschool youngsters
should never become a chore or a drill. The years between two
and five involve great emotional sensitivity, strain and growth.
The child is developing not only his vocabulary and motor abilities but his sense of self and his complex emotional relationships
to mother, father and siblings. Play can be tremendously useful
to the child in working through feelings of rivalry, jealousy and
self-doubt at these ages. But this can happen only if you as the
adult don't overwhelm the child by making the games another
duty or task that must be mastered. Play may be the main
"business" of childhood, but if it's not fun it's not really play.
You need to be able to recognize those moments when you may
be pushing too hard, and back off. A smile, a laugh, a kiss and
a quick shift of direction can make all the difference in the

world in helping the growing child to best utilize what you are offering in play training.

A young child cannot easily grasp the subtleties and difficulties that lie between a wish and its fulfillment. The very young child jumps from the "stick 'em up" of the bandit cowboy toy to its capture by the sheriff on a miniature horse in one quick swoop. This "omnipotent" or "magical" thinking is often considered a basic feature of children's thoughts. But the magic also conveys the child's sense of mystery and wonder about what is strange and new, an interested awe that is one of the most precious experiences we can have. The daydreams of adults can also have some of the magic quality of children's thought. Too often we dismiss this side of ourselves too easily. Helping children develop and expand their ability to make believe may keep that sense of magic alive for them throughout their lives. As those great students of early childhood L. Joseph Stone and Joseph Church have written:

For the adult, music and art and literature and love and even science and mathematics have no meaning without magic. Without magic, we are cut off from our roots in universal human experience and wander forever homeless.

1

Developing the Adult's Imagination

A Starting Point for Training Children

One of the greatest pleasures of being a parent or teacher is the sheer delight of watching a young child grow. In the years from two to five the child unfolds in enchanting complexity, changing from a baby to a searching, curious, emotionally vital and imaginative being. Given a fair chance, most children show this wonderful expansion of intellect, imagery and sensibility. The exercises and parent or teacher interventions in this book will abet and sustain these great possibilities of growth. While childhood is neither naïve innocence nor a blissful golden age, free of conflict, it does have a quality of playful invention that too many adults have lost—or mislaid. One important benefit of working with children is the chance it gives adults to recapture that miraculous sense of wonder, exploration and subtle power over the humdrum world.

Parents or teachers who engage children in the make-believe games or exercises outlined here will discover that something is changing in them as well. As they reach out for the child through empathy and imaginative play, they will find themselves coming back into contact with long-forgotten fantasies, wishes and games, hidden in secret recesses of memory like the little private hideaways under stairs, in attics or in woodland groves children love so well.

Since we now know that the quality of parents' play with a year-old infant is the most powerful determiner of the child's later style of behavior, it follows that the mother or father who can get "in touch" with her or his own playfulness, imaginative resources and childhood joys is much more likely to offer the child richer opportunities for development than the adult who merely provides good physical care, and even love, for the child without exposing him to the whimsy and joy of make-believe. Love, however deeply felt, needs playful actions and words as well, which engage the child's attention and encourage imitation.

Developing Your Own Playfulness

REMINISCENCE: A useful way to begin to open yourself toward playing with children is to regain contact with your own early days. We tend to forget much of our childhood once it is past—the little private games we had, the secret societies, the magical rhymes we repeated, the ritual gestures we used to ward off bad luck, or our scary fantasies about the old house down the street or the ragged old lady rifling the street-corner garbage pails, who might be a witch.

Getting in touch with pictures, events and fantasies of your own childhood can increase your sensitivity to children's thinking and points of view, and may suggest new games to play and rhymes to teach as well. It may also help you enjoy again some of the delights of childhood or see yourself, as an adult, in better perspective.

Think back on activities and memories like these. By reminiscing you may very possibly recapture some of them. Begin by relaxing in a comfortable chair or on your bed and trying to place yourself in the situation of being a three- or four-year-old again. We know that a great deal of the so-called forgetting of childhood experiences occurs simply because we never find ourselves in the right *context*, which arouses such memories. Once you say to yourself, "I'll lie back and be a child for a few moments and let my mind wander," you will be amazed at memories that filter through. The seemingly mysterious effects brought on by hypnotic age regression—in which the hypnotized individual is required to "become" a three-year-old—is simply a more extreme form of concentration that enables memories to flow back. You can accomplish this effectively by yourself, without hypnosis, by relaxing, trying to recall some of the body postures you liked as a child, letting yourself feel like one for a moment, and seeing what images and snatches of early times come to mind.

We ourselves tried this approach as we prepared this material. One of us recalled lying on a cot in a cousin's seemingly mysterious house drinking malted milk out of a baby bottle while two recently arrived immigrant maids jabbered away in surprise that so old a child should still be using a "bottee." The other recalled an incident, sad in retrospect, in which she overheard her parents referring to the apartment-house handyman as a "fairy." Full of awe that a magical creature lived in the building, she confronted him one day in his basement room and asked to see his wings!

Some memories will not be pleasant, of course; teasing, cruelty and threats have always been a part of childhood too. You may remember having your cousins drag you to the bathroom and threaten to flush you down the toilet, or recall an uncle who used to "pull off" your nose and show it in his hand by slipping his thumb between his clenched fist. No one's childhood was all rosy. Though your children or those you work with may not have been subjected to the identical kind of teasing, they are still vulnerable to many kinds of fears and doubts. Your own memories can help you be more sensitive to what a child is going through. You can see how make-believe games of danger and adventure help children gain a sense of control or mastery over the many "real" dangers they believe surround them. And there will remain literally dozens of delightful experiences, wishes, daydreams that emerge. Relaxed reminiscence can start you on the way.

You can also try to get in closer touch with your child's world. Look at the toys, furniture and setting. Think about the records the child likes. Watch the ebb and flow of his play, alone and with other children. You will be surprised at how much more closely you sense what your child goes through from day to day; and this will increase your playfulness with him or her.

DREAM LOG: When we go to sleep at night we are treated to a night-long picture show full of fascinating twists and turns, vivid scenery and the reappearance of long-forgotten friends and relatives. Though many people believe they never dream, recent laboratory research indicates that thinking goes on through most of the night for everyone. Some people, however, remember their dreams better than others. You can train yourself to remember your dreams by the simple process of keeping a dream log or diary. Place a notebook and pen by your bed (and a flashlight if you don't want to switch on the bedlamp). If you awaken during the night, write down quickly and briefly the main points of the dream you just had. Do the same thing on awakening in the morning. The best technique is to lie still for a few minutes upon awakening, playing and replaying the dream pictures in your mind. Then write them down. If you do this for a month you'll have an impressive and intriguing collection indeed.

The object of this dream log is not to look for the symbolic interpretations that are used in psychoanalysis. However, if you keep track of the main characters, the major themes, the occurrence of certain motives such as achievement, power, sex, desire for closeness or aggression, you will also notice facets of your personality, activities or intentions in your life that are not yet fully completed. This awareness can make you more sensitive to other people and to their emotions and motives. The novelty of your own dreams can also help you appreciate the beauty or humor of modern art, fiction and movies. At the same time this sensitivity is helping you personally, it will deepen your awareness of the kinds of material your children enjoy in stories, movies or television.

In addition, keeping track of your night dreams can play a part in assisting you to separate "realities" from fantasies, enhancing your understanding of how hard it may be for a child to make that separation. The young child, under three or four, cannot always tell in the morning whether a night dream was a real event or not. You can explain that dreams are make-believe trips we make at night in our heads, like the make-believe games we play with our blocks and dolls and toy cars and planes by day. In this way you help the child gain a sense of separation between night dreams and reality, and you avoid "putting down" the *inner* reality of the dream. Professor Brian Sutton-Smith has developed the theory that play or make-believe gives the little child a feeling of power in a world of people and objects so much larger than he is. In a sense, being able to label our dreams as dreams and to see them as emanations of our own brain can give adults too a sense of power and control over what often seems mysterious and alien.

The Senoi tribe in Malaysia, which has been studied extensively by the anthropologist Dr. Kilton Stewart, takes its dreams seriously. Within a Senoi family dreams are recounted between parents and children every morning. Dr. Kilton Stewart believes this practice plays an important role in the Senoi's apparent tranquillity and freedom from emotional stress and violent conflict. We know of very little research on whether families that "dream together" thrive or not, but we do know of instances in which the friendly exchange of dreams around the breakfast table introduces a sense of warmth, release and an openness to creativity that parents and children share. It seems worth trying this, if you are inclined, as part of an overall effort to use adult and child playfulness to build rapport and communication within a family. Such morning sharing in school might not be a bad idea for teachers to encourage now and then as well. Many dreams involve danger and distressing situations, of course, or open sexuality, and obviously parents and teachers must employ judicious restraint in what they present to young children.

USING YOUR DAYDREAMS: Almost everybody daydreams from time to time during the day, and just before going off to sleep at night. Once you recognize that such activities are a normal manifestation of the way the brain works to store the vast amount of information it accumulates, you can approach your waking fantasies with the same spirit of playful sensitivity that we have urged for nocturnal dreams. We believe daydreams represent basically the same physiological process as night dreams. Because they occur when we are awake, using our senses and muscles to deal with the environment, they seem less vivid. They also are restrained from too much oddity by our awareness of the physical reality around us.

But our daydreams often carry us far afield, and also suggest recurrent yearnings, the major "unfinished business" of our lives. We can learn to use daydreams too, although a little more discreetly, in suggesting games and make-believe activities for children. Discretion is important because our waking fantasies are often more adult-oriented in their manifest content—as when they represent our wishes for sexual power or sexual explorations with friends' spouses or our co-workers, or our jealousies and envies and greed. In night dreams such themes are often disguised, and represented symbolically. Parents should not use their children as confidants. This can be dangerous, placing too heavy a burden on youngsters, who lack the perspective and emotional stability to cope with complex problems.

Daydreams can be useful if approached somewhat more consciously, in deliberate relation to a specific situation. Suppose it is a rainy day and the children are restless and irritable. Your own fantasies may take you to a Greek island, far from the pressures of daily chores and whining, rambunctious youngsters. Why not make up a game of pretend with the children— a trip to far-off Greece? Think of some of the legends you can remember or pretend you are on a steamer going from island to island and meeting strange adventures on each one. You can use a few household props and help the children develop characters they'll play; and off they go on their own. That leaves you

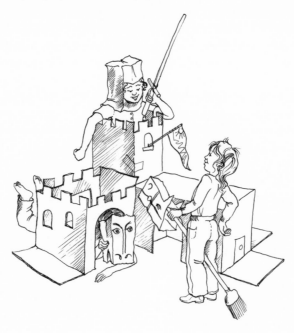

with some time for chores or simply the chance to resume your fantasy.

Daydreaming can add liveliness, color and even intrigue to our lives. It can help us become more creative, in our work and in our social relationships. Our daydreams can even help us in planning for the future. By paying attention to our most outlandish fantasies we may find ourselves asking whether some practical steps toward fulfillment of these yearnings or mental explorations are possible. We can also use our fantasies to calm us. Many psychotherapists and researchers in biofeedback report that picturing yourself in a peaceful natural setting can have a very relaxing effect when you are anxious or angry. And taking a cue from the imaginary companions our children create, we can sometimes overcome the ache of loneliness by engaging in mental conversations with friends or relatives or even our own simulated characters. In Saul Bellow's novel *Herzog*, the hero writes mental letters to famous people: "Dear Winston Churchill . . ." "Dear General de Gaulle." An approach like this can be very useful not only to ease loneliness temporarily but also to stir us into action—writing actual letters and enjoying the increased contact this brings. And don't forget that you can bring your child into this by writing letters to grandma together —or by composing messages to send to the pumpkins at Thanksgiving.

Watching Children and Playing with Them

So far we have stressed developing playful capacities by paying attention to your inner resources, memories, dreams and fantasies. You can change yourself as well by watching children and by playing with them. We have stressed the sheer joy of child-observation. But there is much to be learned from watching how a child tries to cope with the complex environment he or she confronts. The psychologist Kurt Lewin captured the fancy of behavioral scientists the world over in the 1920s with his movies of a toddler trying to sit down on a chair. We take for granted that to sit down, one turns one's back on the chair and eases into it. But as Lewin's films showed, for the one- or one-and-a-half-year-old toddler, turning your back means you don't see the chair anymore: therefore, where has it gone? For the child, the chair doesn't exist when he can't see it. What we take for granted is not obvious to the baby.

Watching your child struggle with problems like these can help you gain perspective not only on what she or he confronts daily, but possibly on some of your own overly rigid and inflexible approaches to situations in your life. You empathize with your child's curiosity and delight as he explores and can ask yourself whether there isn't much that you too can find out if you bring the same attitude of curiosity and wonder to what you do. Watching closely will also help you to decide when to intervene and when to keep away. A good rule is that tasks should have some challenges. Frowns or tears are soon past, and the child moves on in the game or exploration with a greater sense of competence. If you intrude too soon, you'll only encourage dependence.

Playing with your children can be exhilarating. It means putting aside daily cares and worries for a little while and living the gaiety and wonder of the stories and games you work out together. Down on the floor in the doll corner or the pioneer village, you can recapture your past innocence and simultaneously cherish the thrill of being *you*—an adult still capable of fun and excitement. And you can rise from the experience afresh, with a new sense of lightness and delight. We have often observed that therapists who work with children, or kindergarten teachers, or parents who enter into the games from time to time, have warmth and vitality that sober adults with little involvement in children lack. As a partner in play with a child, you are likely to live a richer and more exhilarating life.

Your Role as Parent and Teacher

The readers of this book may be fathers, mothers, grand-parents, baby-sitters, kindergarten teachers, day care center or nursery school teachers or aides, or simply interested adults. Each has a key role to play with children as an *onlooker*, a *participant*, or a *stimulator* or *teacher* of play behavior. Let us take a closer look at these roles for a moment.

ONLOOKER: Watching children is an art in itself. One must take care to be unobtrusive, to blend into the background and avoid rushing out to help pick up fallen toys or even to smooth the edges of a block castle. But parents and teachers do have differing roles as onlookers. In the home the parent or other adult is usually keeping track of only one or two children, possibly with a visiting child or two as well. You can be busy with other things and still pick up a great deal from a child playing in a corner of the kitchen or play area. It is also easy to listen to children's verbalizations in the next room at nap or bedtime and learn a great deal about their play themes or preoccupations.

The teacher has a more complicated task. With a number of children and a higher noise level, it is harder to track a particular child's vocal and behavioral reactions. Still, it can be useful to watch given children for ten minutes at a time, as they weave their way through the group during free play. You might want to notice who initiates make-believe play. How often are there shifts in roles? Does one child always insist on being daddy or Batman? Some children may find a corner and develop solitary play situations. Others will form little groups that stay together for a few minutes at a time. It takes some restraint, but it is probably best at the outset for the adult not to try to force the solitary child into a group, or to interfere when a rambunctious child is seemingly spoiling the game for others. After you have delineated some patterns in the behavior, you can intervene more usefully and offer distraction or alternative game suggestions.

When we train students to be observers for our research projects, we emphasize careful attention to details, asking them to write down almost every move the child makes and every sound or word uttered. We do this to counteract the tendency many young people have toward inaccurate psychoanalytic formulations or overinterpretation of chunks of behavior. The teacher or parent need not go through this exercise, but once or twice it will be useful to you to track a child through the playroom or around the house for ten minutes at a time to see if you can capture exactly what he or she does and says in that time. You will quickly begin to pick up recurring speech patterns, play themes, signs of fear or hesitancy, and indications of just how imagination is developing. If you want to intervene later, you will then have a better sense of what places or games seem to be taboo for a given child, what phrases give a special delight, what level of plot complexity is already developed in make-believe play.

PARTICIPANT: Sometimes children will draw you into a game. Here the art—and it is not easy—is to maintain your adult status while going along with the game. To play at make-believe you may have to unbend a little, imitate different voices or sound effects, or get down on the floor to avoid overwhelming the child by either your size or your better motor coordination. At the same time you have to avoid acting too "childish." A child is confused and distressed if he witnesses adults losing their dignity or behaving like a "baby." You can enter into the game with gusto, but try to play a somewhat more adult role— or at least one in which your size can be employed—as the captain of a ship, a large animal, a friendly giant. Occasionally children, especially the two-year-olds, get enormous laughs from watching an adult play a baby, but this should last only a short time, and you should always indicate to the child how funny the whole situation is.

Here too the role of teacher and parent may differ. The teacher has many other children in her charge. She usually can't take the time to get into an extended make-believe game with only one or two children. The best tactic is to accede to a request to play by stating a time limit, pointing to other children who can later substitute for you, and, again, avoiding too primitive a role in the play. Even more than parents, children in the four-to-five-year age group expect teachers to be somewhat distant or self-controlled.

STIMULATOR OF IMAGINATIVE PLAY: Preschool and kindergarten children welcome an adult as initiator of a game. Most of them have not yet developed enough different story lines or themes and they are hungry for ideas. You can begin by telling or reading a story, or by gathering a set of toy soldiers, utensils, toy cars and planes or blocks. The child needs some structure at the outset, so you might limit yourself to only one story or one game of bus trip and to one special room with a certain set of toys. Children welcome enthusiasm—"This is going to be a really interesting story [game]!"—and other evidence of adult involvement. You should convey to the child as concretely as possible the events in the make-believe plot or the story you are reading. Let yourself go when you imitate train whistles, or Martian voices, or the heroic tones of the captain of the spaceship. The child learns a great deal from such variations in speech and also is delighted by your efforts.

The teacher has a special problem. While successful results can be obtained with half-hour daily sessions with as many as fifteen or sixteen children, the optimal groups are closer to five or six in number. It is important to be sure that the children are reasonably homogeneous in play level. One or two children who are not emotionally ready for group play and disrupt the group by whining, or a combative child who breaks the flow of

the game, can spoil it for everyone. Less concern need be felt
about the occasional child who stays at the periphery and
doesn't get very much into the game. Such a child may actually
be absorbing a great deal, and will reflect it in later play.

Before You Begin

Each chapter of games or exercises in this book exem-
plifies one or more of the benefits of make-believe play we have
described. Every chapter is introduced with a detailed discussion of what the child will gain from the activities. Because
children differ enormously in their patterns of interests, their
motor and vocabulary skills, and their initial response to games
of this kind, we have not divided the book into sections geared
specifically to age. Our experience is that these games suitably
modified will work well with children at all age levels from two
through five. There are games that both two- and five-year-olds
seem to enjoy, though the five-year-old may embroider upon
the original game and add something more. You as the adult are
the best judge of the appropriateness of a game or exercise for
your child. We will suggest the general age group that will enjoy
or understand a game, but we hope you will encourage your
child to explore, become adventuresome and stretch his or her
imagination to the fullest. On the other hand, we urge you not
to expect a group of two-year-olds to act out "The Three Bears"
in the same way a group of five-year-olds will. You will find
yourself doing much of the acting when you read "The Three
Bears" to a two-year-old, yet you can encourage the child even
at this early age to imitate the baby bear's voice and to repeat
some of the words with you.

All the games are adaptable to almost all age groups if you try
to be inventive and if you understand the developmental mile-
stones at each age. *Infant and Child in the Culture of Today*,
by Gesell, Ilg, Ames and Rodell, is a helpful source of informa-

tion about a child's abilities at various ages.

Each exercise can be played with one child or with several children. For teachers we have found that the best group size is four children. Each exercise lasts no longer than ten or fifteen minutes. Before you move on to a new series, repeat the exercises in each unit several times. If you begin with the finger exercises, for example, work with number games for a few days before you go to the color concept of woolen rings. Stay with an exercise until you feel the children have mastered it or have begun to lose interest. You can always go back and repeat a former exercise. We suggest you follow our plan; but certainly you can begin the games at any point in the book, depending upon the abilities of the children you are working with.

Plan to use the suggested books and records (listed in Appendix A) that deal with the material discussed in each chapter, either before you begin the play exercises or as you carry them out. Thus, you might play the record *Birds, Beasts, Bugs and Little Fishes* by Pete Seeger before you begin the animal games. You can also invent your own story for the games we suggest. The appendix is merely a starter. The most important tools for a parent or teacher to have on hand are (1) the desire to participate in being an imaginative partner with the child and (2) a readiness to use everyday materials imaginatively.

Although in general the games and exercises are for all preschoolers, each chapter also suggests which games and exercises are particularly appropriate for a specific age group. Do feel free to experiment. You might want to try some three-year-old games with your two-year-olds just for fun. You may be surprised to see how much the young ones can understand.

2

Preplay: Preparing the Body for Play

Some children move freely, gracefully and rhythmically. Others are more inhibited about using their bodies. The next time you are in a playground observe the differences. While one child seems almost to be dancing as she runs, another moves awkwardly and self-consciously. We have developed some exercises that we feel will help free the child to feel more comfortable with his or her body when he engages in make-believe play.

All exercises can be done with one child or with small groups, preferably three or four children at a time. In larger groups it is difficult to maintain each child's attention; the children also vie for the leader's notice and become more competitive. Our intention in these exercises is to keep competition at a minimum. We view the training exercises as pleasurable, and want each child to feel comfortable with his or her own accomplishments. All age groups can learn to do the following exercises, and you can decide just how much your child is capable of performing before he or she becomes frustrated.

ACTIVITY: **FINGER GAMES**

Fingers become important to the preschool child when he begins to draw, learns to tie his shoes, button his clothes, pull up zippers, feel textures, and of course when he learns to count. The development of fine motor skills in the preschool child will be of help now, as he begins to practice these tasks, and later when he starts school and continues to write letters, cut with scissors, paste, assemble puzzles, color designs and put on his own clothing. Opening his milk container during snack time, cleaning his desk, writing with chalk, catching a ball and countless other fine motor coordination activities will become part of your child's daily repertoire of acts.

MATERIALS

Clay, play dough, wool in assorted colors, ribbons, finger puppets (made of old gloves), felt-tip markers, old sheet or old white dish towels, finger paints (they wash off body and clothing easily)—four colors at least, white shelving paper or finger paint paper, aprons or smocks to protect clothes.

1. Exercise Games

Seat the children around you at a table that has a washable surface. Begin with clay or play dough. Let the children roll the clay into different shapes. Music helps, and we suggest the following chant:

> Rolling my little ball
> Rolling my little ball
> Make it long
> Make it short
> Make it round
> Make it flat
> Roll it back
> Roll it back

2. Finger Counting

Fingers are handy for counting. Why not play some number games and introduce the numbers as the child exercises and plays with his fingers?

Five little fingers [*soldiers, dogs, pussycats, birds*]: Before you begin to play, be sure the children know how many fingers they have, and tell them what they are called. It's easier to begin with numbers rather than names.

There are some old chants and finger songs that one can use with children that make counting fun (see Appendix B). Hold up your hand to demonstrate so the children can imitate your finger movements.

> One little blackbird sitting on a tree.
> Two little blackbirds,
> And now there are three.
> Here comes another one and that makes four.
> Five little blackbirds fly through the door.

> One little doggy, he's all alone.
> Two little doggies, chewing on a bone.
> Three little doggies, scratching on the door.
> Four little doggies, are there any more?
> Yes—five little doggies, sleeping on the floor.

VARIATIONS

Have each child follow your lead in a little finger exercise like this. Use one hand at a time.

1. All fingers are closed and sleeping.
2. Wake them up, one at a time: pinkie, ring finger, middle finger, index finger, thumb.
3. After all fingers are awake on one hand, let them go to sleep, by slowly folding down [in reverse order]: thumb, index finger, middle finger, ring finger, pinkie.

4. Sing softly while your fingers go to sleep, more loudly as you waken them.
5. Now use the other hand.
6. Wake up all ten fingers.
7. Put all ten fingers to sleep.

Repeat the exercise several times until the children learn the names of the fingers. Then let each child take another's hand and wake up his partner's fingers, using one hand at a time, then both hands.

Let the children touch one another's hands: pinkie, ring finger, middle finger, index finger, thumb—first left hand, then right hand.

When you feel the children are familiar with the finger names, call for a finger to awaken out of order: thumb, pinkie, index finger, etc.

3. Woolen Rings

Let the children choose five small pieces of wool, in any colors they want, and help tie the "rings" on the fingers of one hand. Let each child have different colors on different fingers. Tell them:

> All the children close their fingers—and go to sleep.
> Now say: All red rings wake up!
> All blue rings wake up!
> All yellow rings wake up!

Hold up a piece of appropriately colored wool. (This helps the child who doesn't yet know his colors, and teaches color as he learns to move his fingers.)

Each child will be waking up a different finger, depending on which color is wound on each finger. He will have to look at his own fingers, not at his neighbor's, since his "red" pinkie can be another's "red" thumb.

4. Finger Painting

After the finger game above, it is best to do free finger movements again, and finger paint is fun to use. Each child should put on an apron or smock.

Urge the children to spread the paint with their fingers, using long sweeping movements, and with the whole hand. Work on a table with a washable surface. Use finger paint paper or white shelving paper.

After the children have played with finger paints on the table, you might like to try the following:

Spread out an old white sheet or white cotton dish towel on the table. Put newspapers on the floor beneath to protect it. Let each child dip his hand into his preferred color of paint so that his entire hand is covered. Next have each child make a handprint on the sheet or towel in whatever area he or she chooses. Help the children so that their handprints do not overlap too much, yet let them be free in arranging the prints to form a pleasing design all over the sheet or towel. When dry, the sheet or towel makes an attractive hanging for the playroom.

ACTIVITY: **FINGER MAKE-BELIEVE**

MATERIALS
    five animal puppets
    five people puppets

Puppets may be made out of old gloves and scrap materials. Use felt-tip markers to paint eyes, nose, mouth and hair on the glove, or stitch on buttons for the features. Puppets may also be made of paper and Scotch tape to fit the child's finger. Make several puppets, and then help the children develop skits. The adult should lead the way at first. Finger puppets are especially good when a child has to stay in bed.

VARIATIONS

Skit 1.   The Cat and the Mouse
Little pussycat goes to sleep. (Finger folds over and goes to sleep.)

Little mouse comes along and goes "Squeak, squeak." (Little mouse can be on the other hand.)

"Oh," says little mouse. "I can play all I want to now—pussycat is sleeping." (Make the pussy snore.) Mouse suddenly starts to sneeze: "Katchoo! Katchoo!" This awakens the pussycat, who says:

"Who's there? Aha! A nice fat little mouse. Here I come to eat you up."

Mouse runs away. (Put fingers behind your back.) Pussycat says, "Well, well, no one is there. Time to go to sleep again."

Skit 2.   Let's Be Friends
One finger puppet is a little boy.
One finger puppet is a little girl.
Each finger puppet is on a separate hand.

The little boy is singing all alone: "I'm tall as I can be."
(Stretch finger up.) "I'm small as a tiny pea." (Fold finger
small.)

The little girl is walking down the street and nods her head:
"Hello! Hello! Can I play too? "Hello! Hello! I'll play with you."

The two fingers can now be tall, or small, or try to wiggle,
hide in the hand, etc.

Skit 3.   Have You Seen My Dog?

MATERIALS
little boy puppet
little dog puppet
little girl puppet

The little boy and the dog are on one hand, and come out to
play. The little dog runs away. (Finger down and hidden.) The
little boy cries and then the little girl comes. They look all
around the room, or on the bed if the child playing is ill. (Make
big pretense of hunting for the dog.) Then find him in strange
places. (Place finger under rug, on glass or cup, behind a chair,
in the sink, under the pillow.) All three are now happy.

ACTIVITY: **HANDS**

Hands can become anything the imagination chooses
them to be. Tell the children: We've already made handprints
and fingerprints on the sheet and have used our fingers. Now
let's play with our hands.

MATERIALS
old socks
paper bags
scrap material
gloves
lengths of colored wool or ribbon

1. Puppet Games

Children like to use their hands for puppets. Most toy stores sell hand puppets, and they come in a variety of materials—plastic, cotton, paper, rubber. Puppets can also be made out of old socks, paper bags and scrap materials. It is a good idea to have both people and animal puppets. Children love to have princess, prince and monster puppets. So many stories use the hero-and-villain theme that variations on these characters should be easy to make.

You can also make puppet characters that utilize everyday experiences, and represent the policeman, fireman, mailman, bus driver, doctor, shoeman or supermarket cashier. You can even have vegetable or fruit puppets. For example, make a game of things that grow: carrots, apples, bananas, potatoes. The children can puppet-play vegetables and fruits and tell how they pick each one, how it goes on a little truck to the market, how they buy it, put it in a paper bag, bring it home

to wash and clean—and then the climax! The children can tell
how they cook the fruit or vegetable and then eat it—yummy!
And because this is make-believe, they can start the game all
over again with their puppets intact.

2. Hands Are Special—Things They Do

Let the children sit near you and tell you all the things they can
do with either or both hands. Here's a chance for make-believe.
Let's all think!

hammer a nail	bounce a ball
stir chocolate milk	throw a ball
blow a horn	thread a needle
make a cup	make the traffic stop
cut the bread with a knife	make birdies fly
cut paper with scissors	open a jar
make a tent	make an "O"
wind a watch	

3. Right Hand—Left Hand

Most children begin to learn the difference between right hand
and left hand when they start school, although some learn this
sooner. If we wish to help the child differentiate between right
and left, we can do this through the use of color. Children
generally learn the names of colors before they learn direction.
Thus, if we tie colored wool or colored ribbon on their wrists,
we can link the concepts of color and handedness together. For
example, tie red wool on the right wrist, and blue wool on the
left wrist. Then you can say:

"Raise your right hand—the one with red."

"Raise your left hand—the one with blue."

If the child knows his colors, he soon connects the color with
the correct direction. If he doesn't know his colors, we suggest
you do not play games that rely on color or handedness as yet.

Older children can play the games that use either color or handedness.

VARIATIONS

Traffic
Red glove on right hand means *stop*.
Green glove on left hand means *go*.

(If you don't have red or green gloves, paste or Scotch-tape a red or green circle made of construction paper on the palm of each glove.)

The children can make believe they are cars or carts or bicycles and move around the room. One child becomes the policeman or policewoman and holds up a hand. He or she says the name of the hand when commanding "stop" or "go." The children enjoy taking turns at this and learn left and right at the same time.

Roll the Ball
All you need is a pail and a ball. Rest the pail on its side and let your child roll the ball into it from varying distances. The rules are simple. Left hand rolls a ball, right hand rolls a ball. You can keep score for each hand that gets the ball in the pail. This is excellent for developing coordination, as well as for learning which hand to use.

Touch
The children can sit in a circle around you as you instruct them to:

touch your nose   touch a button
touch your toes   touch a zipper
touch a sneaker   touch someone near you
touch your hair   touch someone's socks

4. Shadow Figures

You need a lamp, a wall and a darkened room, or you can hang a white sheet, place the lamp behind it, and have each child take a turn going behind the sheet. The child holds his hands between the lamp and the wall, so that they are seen silhouetted against the wall, or between the lamp and the sheet. Teach the children to make different animals with their hands by demonstrating with your own hands first. They will enjoy guessing what the animal is.

In order to make a crocodile, for example, place one arm over the other and open the hands wide, with the fingers pointed toward each other so that in shadow they look like teeth. To make a bird, link thumbs and flap hands. Dogs, snakes, rabbits, elephants can also be imitated in this way.

The children become more inventive if you say, "Now do a make-believe animal. It doesn't matter if the animal is your very own idea—just take your hands and invent a new kind of animal."

Children also enjoy making the animal's sound at the same time that they imitate its movements. To vary this, the other children can be allowed to make the correct sound of the shadow animal they see before them.

ACTIVITY: **TOES AND FEET**

MATERIALS

Sandbox (outdoors); cardboard or old dresser drawer; box with sand (indoors); oilcloth or plastic sheet (placed under indoor box to catch sand); objects for toe grasping: soft washcloth, plastic cups, clothespin, small rubber ball, wad of cotton; records for dancing and marching (see Appendix A); "tightrope" (chalk line drawn on floor indoors; piece of string outdoors); clay; finger paint; old sheet.

1. Wiggle Our Toes

It's fun to wiggle toes—especially in the sand. Have the children take off their shoes and socks, and sit around on the floor. If you have an outdoor sandbox, let each child take a turn wiggling his toes in the sand—one foot at a time, then both together. If you live in an apartment, a cardboard box filled with sand is a good investment. If you keep it on a piece of heavy plastic or oilcloth, the sand can be swept up and dumped back each day.

Sand and water play are such satisfying experiences for the child that even the most meticulous person might want to allot one small area of the house to "messy" play. If the child is given some simple rules about sand- and water-throwing and is held responsible for cleaning up with adult help, the joys of this kind of play will outweigh the small inconveniences.

VARIATIONS

Picking Up Objects with Toes

Place some small objects on the floor. Ask the children to make believe their toes are little shovels and to try and pick up the objects with toes only. It isn't easy, but it is great fun. With practice the children soon learn to pick up other objects, which they can specify.

Walking on Our Toes

Now suggest that the children walk on their toes in a circle while you play a march record such as "Parade of the Wooden Soldiers." Allow them to improvise. The regular beat of marches makes them easy to follow, but you can alternate them with more imaginative rhythms—waltzes, rock-and-roll, folk tunes and even simple classical music.

Circus Time

Have the children pretend they are walking a tightrope in the circus. Draw a chalk line on the floor, or lay down a long piece of string or old fabric, and let the children walk this "rope," first on their toes and then with the whole foot. Try to teach them to walk backward if they can. The four-year-olds might also try to hop along the line. Show the children how to hold their arms outstretched to balance themselves.

Birds on a Wire

Now let's be birds hopping on a wire (use the chalk line). Sing a little song:

> Hop, hop, here we go
> Hop, hop, here we go
> We are high in the sky
> We are high in the sky
> Watch us as we fly away.

Let the children fly off the "line" and scatter about the room. Call them back and begin again.

Footprints

To make footprints out of clay—Plasticine is best to use because it will harden—have each child step on a large enough piece of clay to make a clear print. When you have a good impression, let the clay harden. The children can paint their own clay footprints when they are hard and dry; remember to tell them they may have to wait a day before the clay is ready to paint.

Footprints, like handprints, can be made on a sheet. Each child dips one foot into a quantity of finger paint placed on a sheet of paper on the floor, then hops—with help—on the other foot to a nearby fresh sheet and stamps on it to make a footprint.

Use as many colors as possible and scatter the children's foot-prints in any pattern. The finished sheet makes a cheerful play-room decoration.

Obstacle Course

You can make a small obstacle course in the kitchen, playroom, child's room or backyard.

MATERIALS

Cereal boxes; large empty carton (about 4' × 4') from toilet tissue, paper napkins or small appliance; large hoop or inner tube from a tire; empty, clean tin cans, painted if you wish (make sure there are no sharp edges); balance beams—one long block placed over two smaller blocks at either end, carefully balanced for stability; tire and heavy cord (to be tied over a sturdy limb outdoors).

Before the children go through the obstacle course, have them help you lay it out in a large room or outside. You can alter the order of the obstacles each day by rearranging the materi-als, but always place them in a large circle.

Place the cereal boxes far enough apart so that the children can step over each one with ease. They can be arranged in a circle or in a straight line.

Next the children crawl "through the tunnel." Use the large carton, with both ends open and the flaps tucked in to lend sturdiness. (Don't cut off the end flaps, because this box can be your puppet theater or tea table at another time.)

Next each child can walk on the balance beam, which can be placed alongside the tunnel or in a line with it.

Then the child moves to a circle made of spaced tin cans. He must tiptoe in and out around each can without knocking it over.

Finally the children walk on the inner tube without falling off. Place the tube so that it is near the cereal boxes. The chil-

dren will have completed the obstacle course by performing each of the five tasks.

You can devise other obstacles as well, such as crawling under an overturned chair or climbing up a small stepstool with adult guidance. The children can also be inventive and suggest their own ideas and materials.

In a backyard, more space can be allowed between each event. A tire can be hung from tree or posts—be sure to use sturdy cord—low enough to the ground to allow a little swing yet permit a youngster to climb onto it and crawl through without too much difficulty.

If you play this game with several children, occasionally you can time each child's passage through the course. You may also keep a record for your own child, to see if he can exceed it each time he plays the game. We do not suggest that you time the children every time they play this game, however, since the prime objective is the pleasure of mastering a skill rather than "winning" a race. Do it now and then, if it suits the temperament of the child and his attitude toward competition.

Make-Believe Feet

Have the children sit on the floor and take off their shoes. Tell them the ways in which feet can let other people know just how they feel.

For example:

a. You walk *fast* across the room—happy, in a hurry.
b. You walk *slowly* and drag your feet—tired, sad.
c. You take big, giant steps—monster feet.
d. You walk on toes—dancing feet.
e. You step forward, step backward—"I don't know" feet or "Should I, shouldn't I" feet.

All of Me

The above exercises are transitions to make-believe body play. Children love to imitate objects and people. We have discovered in our work that they can be truly inventive if you guide them.

JACK-IN-THE-BOX: Have the children sit on the floor. Say: "Let's play jack-in-the-box. Make believe you're in a little box. Put your head down, cover the box, click goes the cover, tuck in your arms, your feet, make yourself small in your box, and now wind up your box and count to three—one, two, three—and out you pop! Ready, back in the box, cover the box, make the lid tight." Repeat.

Change the count each time for the signal for the children to pop out—three, five, four—because the suspense makes the game more fun.

BODY EXERCISES: We like to do a simple stretching and bending exercise linked to make-believe games. The children can bend over to touch their toes if you say:

1. "Bend over, catch ten little butterflies and say 'Hello.' "
2. "Bend over, catch ten little leaves and then blow each one away."

3. "Stretch up tall, reach the stars, catch one if you can."
   (Also use clouds, sun, rocket ships.)
4. "Hop on one foot—be a little rabbit."
5. "Jump, jump, jump, like a kangaroo."
6. "Lie down flat, put your legs in the air and push that cloud away."
7. "Skip to the store, buy some candy, skip home again."
8. "Lie down flat on your back and pedal your bicycle."

DANCING: Your child should begin to feel comfortable with his body when he has played the games outlined above. Now is a good time to explore dancing with him. There are numerous records for children with simple tunes that a child can follow. At the outset, structured games may be better for the more inhibited child. "London Bridge," "Here We Go Round the Mulberry Bush" and "The Farmer in the Dell" are easy movement games to teach. When possible, though, encourage the children to invent their own dancing games. If you start by suggesting that they sit and listen first to the music, then ask them to try and think about what the music sounds like, and *then* encourage them to move, you will see pleasing results. We suggest music that is distinctive, such as marches, music with clearly defined tempo—waltzes or fox trots—music with a quick beat followed by music with a slow tempo, and loud music alternated with soft music.

As the children dance, tell them to make believe that they are:

> a snowflake
> rain falling down
> leaves blowing all around
> a goldfish swimming in a bowl
> a firefly
> a big stormy wind
> a flag fluttering

smoke from a chimney
clothes blowing on a clothesline
a tree bending in the wind
a cloud moving in the sky

The finger, hand, toe and foot exercises should have prepared the child to engage freely in Make-Believe Feet and the subsequent body exercises. Nearly every aspect of make-believe play has some creative elements embedded in it. As the child becomes freer and more comfortable and accepting of his body, he may be on his way to the creation of a dance step, a song or a poem. The following chapters will help you help your child to enhance his play potential further.

Living and Playing Through
All Our Senses

When psychologists talk of imagery they refer to a basic human function, which everyone possesses to some degree. Imagery is our ability to produce again in our minds a response to some stimulation to our sensory organs that occurred in the past—whether that past was a few seconds or months or years ago—even when the original object that produced the sensation is no longer in the environment. Many people tend to think of imagery as primarily seeing pictures in the mind—visual modality. The visual system is perhaps the most highly developed of all the human sensory systems, but the other senses are also involved in producing imagery. We have the capacity to reproduce sights, sounds, smells, tastes and touches as well.

Imagery gives us a haunting power over time; we can suddenly recollect the smell of grandfather's pipe and then recall how we loved to sit on his knee while he told a story. We can recapture in our "mind's nose" the smell of cookies baking, which recalls warm family get-togethers. The joy of living fully through our senses, the taste of good food, the perfume of fresh flowers, the sight of red streaks against the deepening sky of a sunset, are preserved for us by our ability to duplicate them in imagery. We *savor* life, tasting and retasting, seeing and reseeing through imagery.

To enjoy the benefits of imagery the child must first learn to use all his senses fully. Experiencing new sensations requires practice. It takes time for the sensation to develop adequately. If we shift too rapidly from one experience to another, we simply do not *store* the sensations in a way that permits us to recall them through imagery. Therefore it is important that we first build up the range and variety of the child's different sensing capacities. When these are developed, imagery can become a delightful resource for recapturing pleasant sensations.

The potential we have for the full development of all our senses is demonstrated most dramatically by children who are born blind. They have very vivid auditory imagery, and can rehear voices and sounds with greater detail and precision than the sighted person. They also have kinesthetic or tactile imagery to a great degree; that is, they can reexperience vividly movements they have made in the past, or imagine the movements others are making. They can reexperience the feel of something soft or crinkly with a precision that the sighted person is less likely to have developed. The skill the blind show in the development of their other sensory capacities points up the fact that most of us, relying too heavily on our visual orientation, tend to neglect our other sensory channels.

Artists naturally develop their imagery strongly in the area of their medium of expression. One cannot doubt for a moment that Beethoven had remarkable auditory imagery, and long after he became deaf could hear sounds of beauty and power in his "mind's ear." Beethoven had developed his hearing by practice. And so, of course, can the children with whom you are concerned if you will give them the chance. Practice of a full range of sensory responses will lead to richer perceptions at the time they are experienced. Practice also lays the groundwork for improved imagery *in memory*, for reproduction of these

sensations thereafter. Imaginative play draws on the child's capacity for imagery which produces the effects of reality: the
train whistles he imitates, the transformation of a stick into an
airplane. The child who plays make-believe games is both practicing imagery and perfecting his skill at it. The development
of full sensory awareness is the foundation of make-believe as
well as the source of an increased capacity for imagery.

As make-believe games become more complex, they make
increasing demands on the child to introduce elements of sight,
sound, touch or movement imagery. Even older children make
extensive use of make-believe elements as they think about
movies or school incidents or sporting events, filling in details
and sometimes talking aloud to themselves in private.

Imagery skills and good vocabulary often go hand in hand.
Research indicates that children who have well-developed
imagery skills learn reading and vocabulary more rapidly. As
we grow older we tend to rely more and more heavily on
language to communicate and to think, but imagery remains as
important as ever for effective thought, planning and the enjoyment of life. There is even reason to believe that the purely
imagistic aspects of our thinking are controlled more by the
right side of the brain, while the more logical, sequential and
precise kinds of thinking that are associated with language or
arithmetic are governed by the left side of the brain. Despite
this specialization in the hemispheres of the brain, if we are to
live fully in our complex world we need to be able to see mental
pictures or recapture sounds or melodies, as well as summon up
specific words for things. Ideally a person uses both kinds of
skills, for effective communication with others and for the best
kind of thinking.

A child learns about the world around him through his senses.
Infants explore the world through their mouths, and although
they can also hear, touch, smell, and are responsive to changes
in bodily temperature even at birth, the finer discriminations

among the sense modalities appear somewhat later. Watch a toddler's expression when he smells something rancid, or touches something soft.

The "sense" games in this chapter are suitable for all pre-schoolers, though you will want to adapt them according to age. During make-believe, the better the images are reproduced, the more the child will enjoy his play. The cycle becomes complete because as the imagery is reproduced during make-believe, the fact that it is practiced becomes a stimulus to greater recall of new words and stories. The starting point must be the *full* sensing of the sights and sounds, the smell, taste and feel of things. They are the building blocks for the play castles of our minds.

ACTIVITY: **SMELL**

MATERIALS

The newborn baby responds only to the strongest odors, but the young child can learn to discriminate among some common, more subtle smells. We suggest setting up a small shelf with little covered plastic containers (such as clean, empty pill bottles) filled with different ingredients, such as:

cinnamon	coffee	sawdust	onion
mustard	pepper	perfume	vanilla
garlic	tea	peanut butter	pine needles

Before the children sniff these containers, you might want to read them stories about smells and noses. You can also suggest that they look through magazines and cut out pictures of people with different kinds of noses. If the weather permits, the children can go with you to a produce market and smell a wide assortment of fruits and vegetables in season, such as oranges, broccoli, potatoes, bananas, onions, radishes and peaches. At the delicatessen or grocery store they can sniff cheeses, spices, varieties of tea and ground coffee. A trip to the park can yield new items for the shelf, such as dried leaves, a bit of damp earth, a berry or a flower. A visit to the bakery and its marvelous smells of baking bread, rolls, cookies and cakes is a fine way to top off the outing, especially if everyone gets a cookie.

You might want to experiment with cooking to have the children see how smells can change. One easy item to make is yogurt, especially with a yogurt maker. Remind the children that they will have to be patient because it takes time for milk to change to yogurt. Let them smell the milk first, since it will smell and taste different from the yogurt. Add jelly or fresh fruit to vary the basic yogurt smell and taste. The children can even add cinnamon or vanilla from their little containers, and learn something about transformation: spices smell strong when alone and less so when mixed in the yogurt.

ACTIVITY: **HEARING**

Begin with music. You can turn on the radio and let the children discriminate between soft and loud music, fast and slow, and music that conveys moods or feelings. There are books listed in Appendix A that relate to sounds, and we suggest that you read some aloud. There are also excellent records that deal with "noise" and with musical instruments.

The stories and records in the appendix encourage the child to use his ears more resourcefully. Sounds such as the *clinking* of a spoon in a cup or the *tinkle* of an ice cube dropping into a glass, the *swish* of a broom or the *emmmm* of a vacuum cleaner, become more interesting to the alerted child. The books and records also suggest various outdoor sounds, such as wind, rain, the roar of the ocean, and the crunch of snow underfoot. It's fun to look at the pictures or listen to the sounds on the records with your child, and help him imitate these sounds. You will be delighted to hear your child's own variations and his additional "sound" ideas.

MATERIALS

Pop-up-toaster, clock, whistle, vacuum cleaner, horn, bell, electric mixer, running water, egg beater, musical instruments.

Be inventive, and try to find new sounds to listen to each day, both indoors and out.

Let the children close their eyes and guess which of the above items you are using.

1. Make-It-Yourself Band

One enjoyable activity to do with hearing is setting up an impromptu band. Allow the children to make their own "instruments." Some suggestions are:

a. Blow into an empty jug.

b. Fill glasses with water at different levels. Arrange the glasses in a series so that you go from very little water to almost full. Using a spoon, you can then strike each glass. They form a pseudo scale similar to a xylophone.

   c. Bang two pot lids to make noisy cymbals.

   d. Wrap a thin piece of toilet paper once around a pocket comb. If you blow through the paper, you have a home-made harmonica.

   e. Take two blocks and strike them together, or rub them along each other for a nice hollow sound.

   f. Any old pot makes a good drum if you hit the bottom with a wooden spoon.

   g. Egg beaters make nice whirring sounds and are easy for a two- or three-year-old to manipulate.

   h. An old washboard is a useful band instrument if you run a guitar pick or clothespin up and down the ridges.

   i. Large metal spoons struck together can sound like bells.

   j. Take the cardboard cylinder from a roll of paper towels, toilet paper or wax paper, and paint it a bright color. This makes a delightful horn. The children can paste streamers along one side or decorate the "horn" with glitter.

   k. Tie various-size spoons along a strong cord so they are able to dangle freely. Then you can strike them with another spoon and reproduce a glockenspiel.

   l. Take a small glass measuring cup and strike the inside lightly with a metal spoon to make a bell.

2. Guess Who I Am

A favorite game is to listen to one another's voices. Have the children close their eyes before you touch one child's shoulder. The child has to say something briefly, like "Guess who I am" or "I am small" or "I am big," and see if the others can recognize his voice. The children should be told not to disguise their voices.

3. Guess What I Am

Walk around the house or classroom with the children blindfolded, and see if they can pick out sounds such as:

refrigerator humming
footsteps on a staircase
chalk squeaking on a blackboard
water running in the sink

doors creaking
a door or window opening and
 closing
chair moving on the floor

They may need some practice in learning to recognize these sounds, but soon their ears become more sensitive and they begin to guess at other sounds they hear.

4. Outside Noises

Go outside and listen to:

the wind
a bird
a tree moving
a leaf rustling
a ball bouncing

walking on "crunchy" snow
an airplane
an automobile driving along
a twig that is stepped on
dry leaves that are stepped on

5. Music Sounds

Listen to records and recognize music that is:

| loud | fast | happy |
| soft | slow | sad |

6. Animal Sounds

Imitate animal sounds:

| cow | dog | horse | lion |
| pig | cat | seal | rooster |

7. Night Music

Sounds in the evening often scare children. Some books in the appendix are helpful in allaying their fears. It can be fun—and reassuring—to talk with them about the nighttime noises we hear:

ticking clock	crickets
creaking stair	creaking branch
furnace switching on	buses and automobiles
refrigerator turning on	automobile horns
howling wind	sirens (police car, ambulance)
thunder	garbage trucks

8. Make a Telephone

Use two empty, clean frozen-juice cans from which one end has been removed. Puncture a hole in the intact end of each can, large enough to pass a string through. Knot the string ends inside each can so they cannot pull out. Have the children paint the cans if they wish, and the "telephone" is ready.

Pairs of children alternately talk into a can and hold it with the open end to their ear. The string should not be longer than twelve feet if the "telephone" is to work; children enjoy testing the distance to discover the maximum efficiency.

Conversations an adult initiates using the toy telephone are helpful in teaching the child how to play a role. Children also enjoy reversing roles, so in these conversations let the youngster be the daddy or mommy and you the child.

ACTIVITY: **TOUCHING**

The world is too full of "Don't Touch" warnings; it is nice to be able to say "Touch." Children are natural explorers, and if they are given the opportunity to touch, their play becomes much more imaginative.

From the moment he is born, the baby works at adapting to his environment, and the sensation of touch allows him to have contact with animate and inanimate objects. He learns much about his world through touch. Mobiles hung above the baby's crib encourage him to reach out with toes and fingers toward the dangling object. Babies love to touch their bubbles in bath water. One of our favorite memories is the sight of our two-year-old trying to touch a sunbeam coming through his bedroom window while he played on the floor.

Many children enjoy the sensation of touching and rubbing a favorite toy or blanket, or their own ears, noses or hair, while they drink their milk or just before bedtime. Such touching and stroking is comforting to them. It is often a concomitant of thumb-sucking. These are normal occurrences and are related to the child's deep-seated infantile needs for both oral and tactile stimulation.

All children like to pet and touch real animals as well as their toy ones. We can actively stimulate this tactile need in our exercises and games.

MATERIALS

Collect materials of varying textures, such as: velvet, corduroy, feather, cord, absorbent cotton, rubber, plastic, leaf, paper, cellophane, small stones or pebbles, sand or earth, woolen knitted scarves, cork, bottle tops.

Place these items in an old sock, one at a time, and allow the children to put their hands in the sock, *eyes closed,* to feel the material and guess what it is. Vary the collection weekly. Encourage the children to find interesting textures on their own.

1. Let's Touch Each Other

Blindfold a child, let him find another child in the room, and see if he can recognize the parts of the child's body or clothing that he touches—buttons, zipper, hair yarn on a ponytail or braids, sneakers, or a favorite piece of jewelry a child may always wear.

2. Keep a Shelf

Keep a shelf of things to touch and have the children change the items on occasion. Some of the items mentioned above could be kept on this "touching shelf," such as bottle caps, feathers, velvet, etc. As your child finds an interesting object with a texture he or she likes, add it to the shelf.

ACTIVITY: **TASTING**

A tasting tray is probably going to be the most fun of all the sensory experiences—especially if you choose a good assortment of things to eat!

MATERIALS

Sugar, salt, chocolate, cocoa, cinnamon, nutmeg, cooked rice, tea (brewed), orange slice, lemon slice, peeled garlic clove, vinegar, ingredients for applesauce, cookies, bread, etc.

CAUTION

Before you begin this activity, make sure that the children understand that they must never put cleaning items in their mouths or take medicine unless you give it to them. All poisons, insecticides, household cleaners and medicines must be kept *out* of children's reach.

1. Play blowing bubbles to get the children used to using their lips and tongues. They can blow water from a bowl through a straw. A drop of food coloring in the water adds variety. Make lots of bubbles—the more, the better.
2. Have the children taste the foods blindfolded and guess what they are.
3. Bake some spice cookies with the children and let them sample the ingredients as you use them. Have them taste the dough before you bake the cookies, which should be eaten both warm from the oven and after they have cooled.

   You and the children can make applesauce also. Let them taste the apples before they are cooked and afterward. Add cinnamon and call their attention to the change in taste. You can vary the taste of applesauce with a bit of cloves, lemon juice or brown sugar.

When fresh fruits are in season, children enjoy making a fruit salad. They can taste, touch, smell and identify the colors of the various fruits. Add honey or brown sugar or a little cottage cheese or mayonnaise to the salad for variety, and let the children taste the changes that each seasoning or dressing produces.

Vegetable soup can be fun to make as well. Again taste, touch, smell and identify the colors of each vegetable before and after you make the soup. Think of all the new taste and smell combinations you can discover with soup —thyme, oregano, parsley, onion, garlic, dill, chives!

Baking bread is also enjoyable. There are some easy quick-bread recipes. The children will delight in seeing the bread rise and in touching the dough, and of course in tasting the warm bread.

In all these activities, allow the children to help in the preparations within the limits of their skills, and share the cleaning-up chores. They should be participants rather than onlookers whenever possible.

4. Explore your pantry for new taste sensations—and here's a chance to try out *new* vegetables at dinner! A trip to the market is an adventure in tasting, smelling and observation, and the purchase of a new variety to try at suppertime can become part of the game.

5. A good weed guide will tell you what indoor plants and weeds make excellent salads, *if* you are certain you can recognize the edible berries and weeds first.

ACTIVITY: **SEEING**

Eyes tend to be taken for granted. In one game that enhances the appreciation of seeing, each child, blindfolded, explores the room and identifies each object he touches. The world of things to look at is endless, and the objects you choose are up to you.

1. Blindman's Buff

This game all children love is a good beginning exercise for seeing. One child is blindfolded, and has to tag another child in the group to become the next "blindman."

2. Things to Look at Indoors

Suggest that the child look at:

a funny face in the mirror

a bulb growing in a pot of pebbles—measure it each week

a picture book

a terrarium he has helped make

a shelf containing a bird's nest or a bright feather, or dried weeds and flowers

the inside of a kaleidoscope, to see the changing patterns

a piece of colored glass (no sharp edges) to see how objects change their colors when you look through it

colorful sponges

odd shapes of macaroni—shells, bows, elbows

seashells and pine cones in a basket

the contents of a jewelry box—mother's or dad's—to explore the bracelets, rings, cuff links, tie clasps, earrings, necklaces or lockets it contains

a button box or spools of thread

a drop of rain crawling down the windowpane

a snowflake in wintertime as it rests on the window sill

Jack Frost's painting on the window

a mirror he has breathed on, making "clouds"

3. Things to See Outdoors

clouds moving
leaves blowing
branches swaying
moon, stars
sun
insects flying
insects crawling—pick up a stone
   and see the insects under it

a lovely flower
an anthill—poke it with a stick
   and watch the ants scurry
acorns
a squirrel as it leaps from branch
   to branch
"steam" made by the breath
   in winter

4. Games to Play That Use Our Eyes

Ask the children to sit in a circle and show you the object you call for:

> Find all the blue sneakers.
> Find a red shirt.
> Find a brown freckle.
> Find a curly-haired girl.
> Find a button on a dress.
> Find your own ankle.
> Find a pair of blue eyes.

5. Colors

Colors, of course, are one of the first concepts a child learns. As part of our seeing game we suggest you use the names of colors frequently. Sometimes colors have specific meanings for children. In this so-called synesthesia, two sensory modalities are involved—the visual one and a modality such as taste, smell or hearing, which the child attaches to the color. For example, some children see red as "hot" or green as "cold." You can make this into a game by asking the children to associate objects or feelings with colors. In Mary O'Neill's *Hailstones and Halibut Bones*, "Brown is cinnamon and morning toast" as well as "comfortable as love." Green is "lettuce and sometimes the sea" and an "olive and a pickle." Green is also "the world after the rain, bathed and beautiful again."* We have found that five-year-olds respond to these concepts and can become creative poets themselves.

Here are some suggestions:

Ask the children to tell you what "red" means to them and list their ideas on a blackboard or speak them into a tape recorder, so eventually you help them make their own color-meaning book.

Each child can be asked to choose one color for a joint book, or have the child select several colors on his own for an individual book. Sometimes the color naming is more fun if it becomes a shared enterprise, with each child elaborating and adding to the others' meanings.

You can have the children think of blue and name all the things that *smell* like blue. Play music and let the children name the colors that the tune brings to mind. Let the children close their eyes and feel objects and see if they can associate colors to them. For example, a cold glass of water may *feel* "white," or a piece of soft cotton may *feel* "brown." Let the children be free to experiment with their senses and their colors. No one is ever incorrect in this game.

6. Magnifying Glass

Place objects under a magnifying glass and let the children *see* how large and detailed an object becomes. There are magnifying stools with the glass embedded in a small round tablelike surface on legs.

7. Binoculars

Go outdoors and let the children use binoculars, alternating the close-up and distant lenses. They can also look through cardboard cylinders from toilet paper or paper towel rolls.

*See Appendix A.

8. Looking Up

Inside a room, ask the children to lie flat on their backs, heads down on the floor, and look up. Have them describe all the things they see above. Outdoors they can lie on the ground and do the same thing.

9. Looking Down

How powerful it must make a child feel, used to looking up at adults all the time, when he climbs up high and looks down at them instead. With your help and watchfulness, let your child sit on a ladder above you and look down. How funny to be taller! How funny to see the *top* of your head! Let the youngster look down at the objects in his own room and see them from a different perspective. If you are outdoors, the children can look down from atop a Junglegym.

ACTIVITY: **TEMPERATURE**

How do we feel when we are hot? cold? warm?

Fill some bowls with water at different temperatures. Be careful about the temperature of the hot water. Have the children feel the water and tell you whether it's hot, cold, warm.

Take an ice cube and let the children feel the icy cold.

Ask them to tell you where they can feel warm:

near the fireplace	on the hot sand
near the oven	under a quilt
near the radiator	near the dryer
in the sun	in their snowsuits

Ask for places where the children can feel cold:

in the snow
outdoors in the evening when the sun is gone
near the air conditioner

at the North Pole
on an iceberg
when they open the refrigerator
on the skating pond
in the ocean when they swim

Where can children feel cool:

walking barefoot in cool sand
standing near the electric fan
sitting near the ocean
sitting near an open window
drinking a cold drink
washing their faces with cold water or a damp cloth

Make-believe hot and cold:

Make believe we are warm. Show the children how we wipe off our sweat, how limply and slowly we walk, how droopy our body becomes.

Make believe we are shivering. Show the children how they would shake and how their teeth would chatter if they were very cold.

Finally, find pictures of cold objects and places and hot or warm objects and places. Pictures from magazines and travel folders are excellent. A local travel agent will gladly give you a supply. Children will delight in making a cold-and-warm scrapbook.

Magical Changes: Learning About
Ourselves and Others Through Play

Developing Emotional Awareness and Sensitivity

Some of the earliest and most subtle skills we must learn
as we grow up involve understanding the messages we send
each other without words. Our faces, our body positions, and
our hand and foot gestures convey many of our emotions to
others. As adults, we can use that awareness to tell how children
are feeling. A glance at a child's face or posture will give us
important clues. Is the child looking downcast, eyes and head
lowered, shoulders drooping? Is the mouth tight? Is there a
frown? Does he or she walk with dragging feet? Watch the little
girl just given a new puppy. Her face lights up with the upward-
curving wrinkles of a smile and her eyes dance. No words are
necessary, for her "body language" tells us the child's emotions
better than words can.

Children have to discover these clues to others' feelings
slowly and sometimes painfully during the complicated first five
years of life. Learning what facial expressions signal is only part
of the process. It's not so hard for a child to figure out when his
behavior angers mommy or daddy or when it pleases them. But

the next step is trickier—acquiring a sensitivity to another person's feelings so that one can share them and be of help. An important way in which a child learns to develop a sense of self and to become truly human is through this *empathy*.

Pretending and make-believe play can help to further a child's sensitivity considerably. Dr. Eli Saltz's important research with preschool children who had little regular contact with their parents indicated that training in make-believe games could make a big difference in developing their awareness of others' moods. Even when children have a great deal of contact with parents, pretend play can help them pull the different experiences together. Think of the times you have heard a young child saying to a doll or to an imaginary playmate, "Now, now. Don't be a 'fraidy cat. It's just a doggy. Don't be scared because it barks. There—pat its head. Smile! A nice smile!" In this miniature reenactment of his own experience the youngster is often working out his own fears and at the same time elaborating and developing his use of the range of emotions *in context*.

This chapter is designed to help you help a child develop emotional perception and sensitivity by acquiring an awareness of facial and body expressions in other people. When children master these games they will have increased their empathic capacities, and they will also move with ease into the more complex sociodramatic games that follow in later chapters.

ACTIVITIES: **PREPLAY EXERCISES**

1. Faces

Before children learn how to play roles, some practice in the imitation of emotions is helpful. Let the children try simple emotions such as:

happy face
sad face
mad or angry face
surprise
disgust—"icky" face

Demonstrate each mood to the children through your own facial expressions. Cut appropriate pictures out of magazines and hold them up as you talk about a particular emotion; it will help the child understand what you mean. You can also read stories about children who are experiencing these moods (see Appendix A). Thus, by watching you make believe you are sad or happy or angry, and by imitating your facial expression or looking at his own in the mirror, the child learns how to identify expressions of others around him. This nonverbal communication shows him how his friend or mother or teacher feels about something.

2. Expressions

We make a game of facial expressions by asking questions and giving examples:

Tell me, when would you show a "happy face"? Do you think you would be happy to get a new puppy? Show me your face.

Tell me, what kind of face would you make if you got a big box all tied up with ribbons? Show me a "surprise face."

What kind of face do you have when it's raining outside and you can't go out to play? Show me a "sad face."

When your favorite toy gets broken by your friend you get angry. Show me an "angry face." Make up with him and give him a kiss. Show me a "happy face."

Ooh! All the ice cream fell off the table and made a gooshy mess! Show me a disgusted—"icky"—face and clean it all up. Now show me a "happy face."

Use a mirror and let the children see their own expressions as they imitate the different emotions. If you continue with vignettes like these and lead the way, the children become inventive, and soon will tell you stories and suggest the faces that go with them.

ACTIVITIES: **TRANSFORMATIONS**

1. Small Like a Ball—Big Like a Giant

Children are interested in *size*. They want you to measure them. They always ask: How big am I? They have some unusual conceptions of size, space and age, and sometimes think that smaller adults are younger than taller adults.

Ask each child to name his favorite color. Then say: "Become a little red [green, blue] ball. Make yourself all tiny and rolled up tight. Roll on the floor, little red ball, stay very quiet, stay very small. Now become a giant! When I say go, change! Grow tall like a giant. Taller—taller—stretch way up and walk around with big, big steps; make believe you're a great big giant. Take big steps."

Playing music with these games increases the fun. You can chant if you have no music available.

> Small like a ball [repeat]
> Tall like a giant [repeat]

What other things are small? Ask the children to turn themselves into other small things, then alternate with big ones.

> Small like a pebble
> Tall like a mountain
> Small like an apple
> Tall like a tree

The children can take turns while you repeat the chant. "Make yourself very small, roll yourself up very tight. When I say go, change!" "Make yourself very tall, way up on your toes —go!"

2. Blow Me Up

Have each child choose a partner to "blow up" like a balloon. As the child blows—puff, puff—on his partner's back, the "balloon" pretends to get bigger and bigger and then to float around the room. All the "air" is let out, and down goes the child in a heap. Have the children take turns at being "blower" and "balloon."

3. Change Your Shape

Use an old single or twin-size bedsheet. If you cut slits in it, the child can see where he is going. Demonstrate the game first, by draping the sheet over a child and letting him move any way he wants. He can make different shapes by shifting his hands, legs, head, body. Let each child crawl, walk, roll, move in all directions. You can let two children go under the sheet together, as long as it doesn't get too wild.

4. Let's Be Animals

This game is best if you read stories about animals before you begin to imitate them, and show the children pictures you have cut out of magazines.

The animals in this game all have different kinds of movements:

> horse—gallop
> cat on the fence—walk, leap and climb
> dog—walk and run
> kangaroo—jump
> snake—crawl along the ground
> elephant—swing arms in front for a trunk
> fish—swim on the floor and jump for a worm
> bird—fly high in the sky
> lion—stalk around and roar
> seal—flip arms as "flippers"
> caterpillar—inch along the ground

Have the children make believe they are at the zoo or in the barnyard, and let them take turns visiting each animal, to feed and pet it. They can make animal noises too. The game can be

carried as far as the imagination of the child allows: Take the dog for a walk, feed the elephant, ride on the horse, have the seal do tricks.

5. Be Anything but Yourself

The charming book *Whee! I Can Be* is good to use right here. Children can act out the parts in the book, such as an elephant, leaping like a bunny or flying like a plane. Playing statues with music is also fun. Play a record, stop the music and let the children "freeze" into any animal shape or person they want.

6. Bag of Hats

Children like to pretend that they are animals, magical characters, heroes on television, their favorite cowboys or sometimes their mothers and fathers. When Cowboy Joe is wearing his worn-out cowboy hat, there's no use calling him by his real name; he won't answer until you call him "Joe."

Preschoolers also like to change objects around them into other things. Whenever you witness make-believe play you will see transformation taking place. A box becomes a table, a cave, a room, a tunnel. The wearing of a hat changes a child into another person. Here are some suggestions to help generate transformation of self and objects. These are merely outlines, to be changed and elaborated upon as you choose.

MATERIALS

Collect as many hats as you can, for a nurse, baseball player, policeman, fireman, train conductor, cowboy, sailor, farmer; and for home roles, a lady's hat, a man's felt hat, cap, gardening hat. Place the hats in a big basket and let the children choose one at a time. When they put on the hat, help them act out the character as suggested below. You can also encourage the children to make hats using construction paper, Scotch tape or a stapler, and your scrap bag. Taping ornaments onto paper hats can be fun.

BASEBALL HAT: "Here's our famous hitter. See his bat, watch me throw a ball." Call out, "Strike one, strike two." Then let the child hit a "home run," and make believe the ball flies high. Encourage the other children to cheer and to follow the imaginary ball with their eyes, while the "hitter" runs home safely.

GARDENING HAT: The child can "fill" a make-believe watering can, sprinkle the flowers, smell them, pick some and give them to a friend.

NURSE'S HAT: Make believe one child is ill. Ask the nurse to look at his tongue, feel his forehead, take his pulse and advise, "Take this medicine and you'll be all better."

FIREMAN'S HAT: "Put on the hat—we all smell smoke. Pull the alarm and wait. Here comes the fire engine." Make loud siren noises. "Mr. Fireman, get your hose, the little house is burning down. Save my dog, save the family—please save my favorite toy. Hooray, the fire is out!"

SAILOR HAT: "The sailor is on his ship—and the waves make the ship roll like this [move from side to side]. He sees a whale. He sees another ship. He looks through his spyglass [cup hands]. He sees some land, land ahead. Drop anchor and put him on the little gangplank. Back on land again."

DADDY'S, MOMMY'S HAT: "It's morning. Daddy [Mommy] wakes up, gets dressed, eats breakfast, puts on the hat and says goodbye. He [She] gets in the car or the bus and goes to work." The child sits in a little box and makes believe mommy or daddy is driving or sitting on a bus or train. Lots of familiar sights can be passed on the way—the school, the church, the stores, the river, the factory.

7. Magician

MATERIALS

All you need are a long cape made of a piece of inexpensive black crepe or rayon, a big safety pin, a wand (a chopstick saved from a recent Chinese dinner) and play dough or soft modeling clay.

The magician is named Mr. Magic. He can do anything! First demonstrate how the game is played. Put on the cape, take a small piece of clay, roll it into a ball and say: "This is an apple —do you think Mr. Magic can change this into a banana? Well, *close your eyes* and say the magic words: 'Abracadabra, one, two, three.' " While the children have their eyes closed, roll the clay out into a banana shape. "Open your eyes and here's the banana!"

Allow each child to take a turn. You will have to help with the clay shaping, but let the children's imaginations call for whatever they want. To them the clay will look exactly like their imaginings:

> ball into snake
> banana into dog
> leaf into flower
> plum into cat
> ring into ball
> apple into octopus

8. Development of Sequence

Children from two to five become increasingly aware of the weather and the seasons, though they may still believe in what the renowned child psychologist Jean Piaget has called *artificialism*—that there is someone up in the sky who makes the rain or snow. We suggest some imaginative games based on the weather.

MATERIALS

You will need pieces of crepe paper about six feet long and three feet wide, so that four children may fit comfortably underneath. Buy white, blue and orange paper to represent winter, summer or spring, and fall respectively, and gray paper for rain. You also need some thumbtacks and two tables placed about five feet apart. Take a piece of crepe paper and tack an end to each table, stretching it to make the "sky." Tell the children to sit down on the floor between the tables, under the "sky," and make believe it's the appropriate weather and season.

BLUE SKY: "It's summer or spring. What do we do? We put on our bathing suits and we swim. Everyone swims. [Move out

into the room for more space to perform each activity.] Come back under the sky. What else do we do when the sky is blue? We roller skate. We ride our bikes, we swing, we lie in the sun on the beach. We put on the sprinkler. We plant flowers and vegetables, water them, pull out the weeds."

GRAY SKY: "It's raining. Put on your boots, your raincoats. Let's splash in a puddle. Make a little paper boat, and let's have a boat race downstream. Put up your umbrella. Jump over the puddle. Catch some rain in your pail. Wash your face! Taste a raindrop."

WHITE SKY: "It's winter and it's snowing. Put on your snow-suits, boots, mittens, woolen hats, mufflers. Ready? Let's go sled-ding/go skiing/throw snowballs/make snowmen/make snow angels/get our shovels and shovel the path/ make some snow cupcakes/write our names in the snow."

ORANGE SKY: "It's autumn, and all the leaves are making the sky look orange. Catch the leaves when they fall. Pile them up. Skip on them, hear them crunch, crunch. Watch the wind blow the leaves. Make a great big pile—higher, higher, to the sky. Jump in it. Cover my legs with leaves. Bring home a colorful bunch for the table."

9. Airplane Game

MATERIALS

You will need a collection of assorted colorful chiffon scarves bought in the ten-cent store, a story about an airplane trip, some boxes or cushions that can become seats on the plane, a hat for the pilot, and a hat and trays for the stewardess.

Discuss with the children the sequence of events involved in taking a plane trip: purchasing a ticket, weighing the luggage, boarding the plane, fastening seat belts. Make an airplane by arranging boxes or cushions in two rows. The pilot should sit up front, and one child can be the stewardess. She or he checks each seat belt and gives each person a tray of "dinner."

The children make believe the airplane is flying and they can go anywhere in the world—for example, the zoo. They can imitate the animals they might see there—lions, bears, penguins, elephants. Or they can make believe they arrive at the North Pole, where they are cold and shiver and shake and look for igloos, polar bears, seals and ice floats. Other places to land

are a toy factory, candyland, a jungle or a farm.

The children can become airplanes too. Let each child choose a scarf from the bag of chiffon scarves, hold it by a corner and sit on the floor in a circle. Say to the children, "We are going to make believe we are airplanes. We can fly anywhere in the world. When I say go, pick up your scarf and get up and move around the room. You can go fast or slow, up or down, and when I call out your color, come in for a landing."

This game is fun outdoors, where there is more space for moving freely and the wind can pick up the scarves and billow them out. The children can improvise their movements, and make sounds like jet engines.

5

Poems, Songs and Stories: Paving the Way for Creativity

It is natural for preschool boys and girls to talk aloud when they play at make-believe. Piaget called this *egocentric speech,* since two children standing side by side, each describing his or her particular fantasy game, may not actually be communicating with each other. By talking aloud, children hear their own speech, and this provides them with an intriguing set of new sounds and words. The games in Chapters 2 and 3 were designed to prepare the child to sharpen sensory awareness, and to develop a number of different words to describe experiences. When the child uses sounds and words in new combinations as he plays, he learns additional ways of expressing himself.

Of course, what youngsters say aloud doesn't always come out quite "right" from an adult's point of view. The quaint or "cute" sayings of boys and girls which delight adults often derive from the children's efforts to use sound effects or adult remarks before they fully understand their meanings. A boy we know pretended to drive around in a truck selling ice cream. He was playing "college," he told us, because "Daddy said he was a Good Humor ice cream man when he was in college." A four-year-old girl lined up all her toy cowboys and soldiers "to rescue my daddy" after hearing her mother comment that father would be late for supper because he was "all tied up at work."

Although we may laugh at the child's stumbling efforts to comprehend or use new words or phrases, we are likely to correct mistakes gently and thus help the child improve the effectiveness of his speech. Make-believe play gives him a chance to try out overheard phrases and correct them, or to reshape them as the game takes new directions or as adults or other children react to what he or she says. Often, playing with other children exposes the child to new word combinations and sounds or expressions. Shared make-believe games can therefore be very rewarding learning experiences in vocabulary-building, as Piaget has pointed out.

When children do play together, they suggest new words or new roles to each other. In groups of two, three or four youngsters, we hear them saying:

"Make believe you're the mommy, I'm the daddy and you're the baby."

"Make believe I'm the princess and you're the prince, and *she* can be the bad witch!"

"Let's play train. You be the conductor. You know, the one who takes the tickets."

Some children seem to have a keen ability to shift and change roles and to enter into make-believe play without any difficulty; others are more self-conscious. They hang back, appear to be passive in their play, and accept the role thrust upon them by their more imaginative playmates. Almost all children enjoy make-believe and try it out for themselves, but some shy or passive children need adult help in developing the *content* to be used in games or the *courage* to try things on their own.

In some of our recent research, a teacher met for half an hour each day with a group of four-year-olds and started them off with make-believe games such as Pirate Treasure Hunt or Airplane Ride. We noticed that one child rarely participated in the puppet, magic or animal games we played although she did sit close to the teacher and watch her intently. We had been observing this girl during the play periods before we began the project, and her ratings on spontaneous imagination were low. She played alone with structured toys like plastic molds or jigsaw puzzles, or followed a playmate who was engaging in motor activities such as riding a bike, skipping or piling blocks up neatly. After her two-week exposure to the "play lady," she was again observed during free play. We watched her playing house. She sat at a bare picnic table with three little boys. "All right, now eat your dinner," she told them. "Everybody eat up. Here's food for you, food for you, and food for doggy." She leaned down and gave an imaginary dog imaginary food.

For this child dishes, food and even a dog now existed. She was playing mother and these were her three children, her doggy, her kitchen. After the "meal" she led the three boys and the "dog" across the lawn to a little hill which she called the "living room" and where she now let everyone "read and watch TV."

We were delighted and surprised. Evidently this child had always had the capacity for make-believe. All she needed was the sanction from an adult that pretending was acceptable. Her play thereafter continued to be inventive, freer and filled with make-believe components.

This example demonstrates that many children have the basic ability for make-believe but need some form of encouragement before they can move easily into such play. Too often, parents may not realize that by ignoring the quiet child they are holding him or her back from exploring imaginative games. Too often, too, the tendency is to let TV serve as a playmate when the mother or father could stimulate so much activity in the child if they took a few minutes a day to initiate a little make-believe play. As our example suggests, the shy and passive girl not only found herself playmates, but she was trying out more words and enriching her vocabulary and imagery, and developing her self-assertiveness.

This chapter aims to open the door to make-believe by providing children with interesting *material* for play—new words, rhymes and songs—as well as giving them *sanction* and encouragement. Poems, stories and songs are useful because they provide a more clear-cut format, a structure children can follow easily. Our experience suggests that the rhythm, rhyme and definite story line of these materials hold the children's interest better than unstructured material. Once they play through them a few times, with you and on their own, they will move on to trying the words they've heard and the parts they've played in new settings of their own creation. This paves the way for them to develop their own originality more fully.

If you have played some of the games and exercises in the preceding chapters, you can now begin to teach make-believe games. Remember, not every child needs to be taught. You will have to use your judgment about your own child's imagination. You may need only to suggest that he or she play fireman and the child will go ahead and do it. But you may have a child like the little girl described above who needs some help and encouragement from you. This chapter is designed to help both kinds of child.

ACTIVITY: **POEMS**

You may find it easier to start with poetry instead of a story or song. Most children know nursery rhymes, and if they have gone through some of the exercises described earlier, they have already tried bits and pieces of make-believe. Begin with a simple poem that your child knows well and encourage him to act with you.

"Little Jack Horner" is a good poem to start with. As you recite the rhymes, go through the motions—first by yourself and then along with the children.

Little Jack Horner
Sat in a corner
Eating a Christmas pie.
He put in his thumb
And pulled out a plum
And said, "What a good boy am I!"

Actually sit down in a corner and make believe you're eating, using exaggerated movements of mouth and tongue, licking your lips, taking pieces of imaginary food to your mouth. Then, very slowly, put your thumb into the "pie" and pull out a "plum." Show it to the children, using your hands to indicate how round it is. Then comes the climax. "What a good boy am I!" Pat yourself on your head. Clap your hands. Put your fingers through imaginary suspenders and wiggle them in pride.

1. Little Miss Muffet

"Little Miss Muffet" is a natural follow-up because many of the movements are the same. This time you and a child will play together. Take turns being the spider, and try out all variations of crawling and scaring "Miss Muffet away." Children have grown up with these nursery rhymes for generations, and the element of scariness in the spider is greatly reduced by acting out the poem and by the mastery over his fears that develops as the child repeats the rhyme and acts it out.

2. Little Boy Blue

Little Boy Blue,
Come blow your horn.

Imitate a horn by cupping your hands to your mouth, and say, "Toot toot."

The sheep's in the meadow,
The cow's in the corn.

You can get down on all fours and imitate the sheep (Baa, baa) and the cow (Moo, moo).

> Where is the boy
> Who looks after the sheep?

Pretend you are looking for him—under the chair, under the sofa, behind the door; here the game can have endless variations.

> He's under the haystack—
> Fast asleep!

Here you stretch out and snore and snore and snore. This rhyme is great fun for three or four children. Each can take turns being the boy, the animals, the horn, and making the tooting and snoring noises, and everyone can engage in a long search for the little boy.

3. Make Your Own Poem

Suggest to the children that they talk about something they would like to do, or that they did the day before, which you will help them make into poems. Perhaps their poems will be inspired by a trip they took, a story they read, a pet they own. Encourage them to say their thoughts out loud and with rhythm. Even if the rhyming is not perfect, two or three lines will make a simple poem. You can write them down, and let the children illustrate them in a little scrapbook, pasting the poems on construction paper, and fastening the papers together with staples or brass fasteners. Poetry ideas can be simple:

> Food to eat
> A pet I own
> What I see from my window
> A wish I made
> Who lives in a hole?

Things that fly in the sky
People I love

If you make up the poems at first, and give the children some simple rhyming words, they will quickly get the idea. Ladders of nouns generally help them get started. For example:

red	green	nest
bed	bean	rest
head	blue jean	best
sad	book	wheel
bad	cook	heel
had	look	feel

Show the children how they can combine new words with the ladder words:

I put a green bean
In the pocket of my blue jean.

A little bird will rest
In his warm, snuggly nest.

4. Songs to Act Out

Songs are a fine alternative to poetry. Most children enjoy singing, and act out songs just as easily as poems.

Begin with "Row, Row, Row Your Boat."

The words are repetitive, and enable the child to sit on the floor and imitate rowing movements vigorously without having to worry about intricate lines to sing.

You can act out the song with one child, or with pairs of children, who can hold hands while sitting opposite each other, rocking back and forth.

If you wish, use records (see Appendix A) with one child or a small group and let them act out the songs. The children can skip, walk on tiptoe, swing and toot to all the lively tunes on the records. Playing records that deal with feelings and body movements can help children express a variety of emotions. They can smile, frown, giggle, shake, rub, bend and turn. The Mother Goose nursery rhymes are found on many records and you can play these while you act them out with the children.

5. Movement Game

Using record music in the background, you can show the children how to:

> ride a horse
> drive on a bumpy road
> be a ballet dancer
> conduct an orchestra
> ride a bicycle down a hill
> catch an ocean fish
> imitate a flying seagull

You can use music as background for acting out a visit to a haunted house, with green goblins mixing a mysterious brew, witches flying on broomsticks, black cats scurrying across the room. Or you can have the children act out a space trip: making believe they are rocket ships taking off, then landing on the moon, moving slowly as if they had no weight, discovering odd moving objects and strange creatures, pretending they are exploring outer space while still attached to their rocket ships.

A game can be made of an imaginary ocean voyage. The children can imitate the noises of the wind, the movements of the waves, the rocking of a buoy and the sound of a ship's horn. They can land safely near an island and explore it, dig for treasure, build a lean-to, look for food, go fishing in the ocean, cook their catch and imitate noises of strange birds and animals.

6. Acting Out Stories

If your child has tried to act out some songs and poems, you can become more ambitious with some simple stories involving one child or three or four at a time. Be sure to tell or read the stories aloud several times first.

GOLDILOCKS AND THE THREE BEARS: A familiar tale is much easier for the child who is playing at a role for the first time. He is less self-conscious if the story is part of his world. With "Goldilocks," you might proceed like this:

"Once upon a time, there were three bears. The papa bear [stand up; look very big and strong], the mama bear [smile and make believe you are at the stove cooking, or pretend to sew, or use simple props like a hat or a pocketbook] and the baby bear [have a toy or bottle and use a tiny voice]."

Continue with the story, telling about the hot cereal. Let each bear taste the cereal and say, "It's too hot!" Papa Bear decides to go for a walk in the forest and Mama Bear and Baby Bear go too. You and the children can act this out quite easily.

While they are gone, along comes Goldilocks. You can first show what Goldilocks does: tastes the cereal, eats it all up; sits on each chair, breaks baby's chair; tries out each bed, falls asleep on baby's bed; and then let the children play the parts.

Then the bears come home and the excitement mounts.

Enact the scenes of discovering that:

> the food is gone
> the chair is broken
> at last they find Goldilocks

We prefer the version in which Goldilocks is invited to stay for dinner rather than being chased away—but try them both!

PING: Another story we like to act out is *Ping*, by Marjorie Flack and Kurt Wiese (Viking Press, 1933).

Ping is a duck. (Here's a chance for lots of quacking!) Ping lives on a boat on the Yangtze River. Ping marches every day across a bridge to the shore. It's fun to line up Ping and all the little "ducks" and let them all march along, going "Quack, quack."

Show how they hunt for snails and fishes. When sun sets the master calls "La-la-la-la-lei," and the ducks march back. Last one back gets a spank on the back.

One day Ping does not hear the call. He doesn't want a spanking and he hides. Show how the children can hide under the sofa or behind the door.

The story describes Ping's adventures the next day. He sees dark fishing birds. Show the children how to fly and swoop down.

Then Ping sees some crumbs on the water. Ping sees a little boy with a barrel on his back which was tied to a rope from his boat. Show the little boy swimming in the water.

The little boy has a rice cake. Ping snatches the rice cake. This can be done with great excitement. The little boy screams and grabs Ping. Ping quacks and quacks.

The little boy's family hears all the noise and pulls the little boy and Ping out of the river. This gives everyone a chance to playact together.

The boy's father wants to cook the duck for dinner. "No!" says the boy. But the father puts a basket over Ping.

The little boy quickly comes to Ping, takes off the basket and drops Ping back into the water.

Ping hears the master's call: "La-la-la-la-lei," and this time decides to go up the bridge. He is last; he does get a spank on the back from the master. But he's glad to be home with his mother and his father, his two sisters and three brothers and his forty-two cousins.

CAPS FOR SALE: *Caps for Sale,* written and illustrated by Esphyr Slobodkina, is one of our favorite books. This is a delightful tale for playacting with a group of children. The story is simple. A peddler carries all his caps on his head and walks through town calling, "Caps for sale. Fifty cents a cap." He walks until he gets tired, sits down with his back to a tree trunk, still wearing all his caps, and falls asleep. While he sleeps, some monkeys take his caps, put them on their heads and climb back into the tree. When the peddler awakens he sees all his caps on the monkeys' heads. He shouts and yells and tries to get them back, but the monkeys will not throw down the caps—until the peddler throws his own cap down on the ground in disgust and the monkeys imitate him. Then he places them on his head once again, and goes about his business, calling, "Caps for sale."

All you need are some old hats. Try to get as many as you can. If you are playing this game in school or at home in the winter, it's no problem since your child's visitors or the children at school all have their own. Choose the peddler and pile the hats on his head, one on top of the other. All the other children are the monkeys. Let them hide in the room. Make a big issue about keeping very still and hiding very carefully until the peddler falls asleep.

Now begin the playacting.

Let the peddler say, "Caps for sale, caps for sale. Fifty cents a cap." Let him walk all around the room, repeating his call several times. Then with much yawning and stretching, the peddler can show how tired he is, lean against the wall—his tree —and touch his caps before he goes to sleep to make sure they are all there. He can even say this out loud.

Now the fun begins. Have each "monkey" tiptoe over one at a time, slowly take a hat off the peddler's head and run away. They make believe they climb a tree, and sit together on the couch. Remember to leave *one* cap on the peddler's head.

The peddler wakes up, touches his head and discovers his caps are gone. Let him be surprised, say, "Where are my caps?" and look all around.

Next he can look up and say, "You monkeys in the tree, give me back my caps."

Have all the children imitate the peddler, shake their fingers at him and go, "Tsz, tsz, tsz."

You can elaborate on all the ways in which the peddler begs for the return of his caps. Be sure to have the monkeys imitate every movement the peddler makes. This helps reinforce the idea of imitation.

Finally the peddler throws down his own cap in anger. And now comes the grand climax. Each little monkey imitates the peddler and throws down his cap in the same way.

The peddler picks up all the caps. He can mention the colors as he puts them back on his head, and when they are all piled high on his head again, away he goes, calling, "Caps for sale. Fifty cents a cap." Depending on the age group, you can elaborate each segment of the little tale, adding such elements as the number of caps, their colors, and the special way each child puts on his cap.

We suggest you go very slowly at first in playacting. Repeat scenes over and over, and leave out some of the descriptive material if necessary. Once you begin playacting, the children will all want to act out their favorite stories. This is a good rehearsal for the sociodramatic play described in the next chapter. Familiar stories help children to become freer to draw on their own power of inventiveness. They are then ready to act out their own made-up stories, or act out recent events that happened in their lives, such as:

a birthday party	a picnic or bus trip
a visit from grandma	a visit to the firehouse
getting a haircut	a trip to the aquarium

ACTIVITY: **PUPPET SHOW**

MATERIALS

Large box (about 4′ × 4′), card table, tablecloth or sheet, scrap materials for curtain, dowel or rod, puppets, floor cushions.

Use a large empty carton for a stage, with the end flaps folded in for support. Place the box on a card table covered with a long cloth or sheet, so that the puppeteers can sit on the floor behind the table and not be seen by the audience. The idea is that the puppets be held up high in the open box so that they are visible to the audience, while the puppeteers sit hidden, working them.

If you wish, the children can paint and decorate the box and hang a small divided curtain from a dowel or small curtain rod at the front. Thrust the ends of the rod through the sides of the box near the top. The children can easily separate the curtain and move each half aside before the show begins.

Place chair cushions in front of the puppet stage for the audience and have the children help make paper tickets and paper money to create a theater atmosphere. They can even prepare a simple illustrated program. The music can be furnished by the kinds of instruments described in the Make-It-Yourself Band on page 53.

The puppets can be made of papier-mâché, old socks, mittens, or old rubber balls placed on a stick. Puppets can also be bought in the dime store, but it's more fun to make them together and is indeed a fine activity for a rainy day.

Some of the ideas we described in this chapter can be acted out with the puppets. Puppets can sing, recite poems and enact nursery rhymes or the simple plots suggested above. Once you begin, the children will invent their own plots, and at each show they will enlarge and change the story line. We find that some children feel less inhibited about acting out a story through manipulation of the puppet characters than they are by playacting themselves. If this is the case, you may want to use the puppet show device earlier in this chapter, when you begin the rhymes and songs.

New Roles and Social Situations: Sociodramatic Play

Once children between the ages of two and three have mastered the rudimentary aspects of walking and talking, they are ready for a new and exciting adventure—confronting the complex and subtle social environment in which we all live. Make-believe play is an important means by which the child can begin to identify and to "try on for size" the varied and sometimes confusing social roles that characterize our culture. In every culture throughout the world that anthropologists, psychologists and sociologists have studied, one finds a series of clearly defined roles that children and adults are expected to play, some parts more appropriate for certain ages than others, some assigned more to one sex than the other, some associated with survival and work, some set aside primarily for recreation or for the spiritual and cultural aspects of living. The preschooler in our society begins to learn that there are certain kinds of behavior and ways of walking and talking that are "grown up", some that are "mommy" or "daddy" roles, some that are "childish." There are also other grownups who have special roles (often but not always associated with particular costumes), such as the doctor or nurse, the policeman, the mailman, the schoolteacher. Through the further stimulation that comes from storytelling and especially from television, there are the imaginative roles of adventurers, soldiers, spies, athletes, supernatural figures, and queens and kings. Each of these roles has certain defining characteristics—adults are bigger than children; nurses, policemen and athletes usually wear special costumes—and some roles have strictly defined rules or conventions associated with them.

As an adult you play a critical part in how the children with whom you are associated come to identify and to understand the varied roles available in our culture. Your own behavior in your major role for the child—as parent or teacher—is of course especially important. But you also interact with other adults— the mailman, the storekeeper, the appliance mechanic, or the parents of other children—and the children observe you in these relationships. You demonstrate by your facial expression, tone of voice and gestures, as well as the comments you make afterward, something about the importance or the acceptability of these roles. The kind of make-believe games you play, the roles you assign or take on yourself with your child, can also be very important. Helping your child to play sociodramatic or make-believe games provides a basic skill which he can use to prepare for his own social roles. It also gives you a chance to identify problem areas in the child's grasp of these roles which you can then deal with.

For the preschooler, the first clearly defined role to grasp is that of child versus grownup. Simultaneously, the child is also inculcated with the society's views of "appropriate" boy or girl behavior in hundreds of subtle and direct ways. Today we are in the midst of an important transition in our society, from one that differentiated sharply between behaviors appropriate to males and females to one that accepts a much greater overlap in the kinds of tasks and careers open to both sexes. A few years ago, very careful research by Dr. Greta Fein of Yale University

indicated that mothers who played actively with their eighteen-
month-old daughters had already influenced them toward
enacting the more traditionally female role of feeder or care-
taker, while they had encouraged their sons to play "adventure" games. If you are serious about preparing the children in
your care for a society in which a greater diversity and overlap
of activities for both sexes are desirable, then you can begin to
stretch the old-fashioned role assignments by letting boys be
free to play make-believe games with dolls and girls take on the
role of doctor or spaceman when they want to. Actually, research has indicated that over the past fifty years girls have
been moving steadily into playing more traditional boys' games.
Parents can help boys prepare for a new pattern of sex-role
relationships by allowing and encouraging them to play at
being cooks, caring for children, or being the school teacher or
nurse as well as the cowboy and the doctor.

A four-year-old named George was playing Daddy Goes to
Work at nursery school. He wore a man's hat and had a woman's
pocketbook over his shoulder. Both of George's parents work.
Here George was identifying with daddy, but he also was attempting to assimilate his mother's role into his playtime by his
use of the purse. In his play he included both daddy and
mommy in his imitation of household chores such as cooking
and doing the dishes. Then the daddy figure got into a "car"—
a plastic cube turned upside down—and drove off to work with
lots of noisy imitations of horns blowing, motors rumbling and
"bye-bye" waves. As we observed George over a period of time,
his primary identification was with daddy, but his play reflected
the roles he had seen both his parents enact.

The advantage of sociodramatic play is that the child who
tries out a great range of roles and has an extended store of
make-believe for his play will be better prepared for novelty
and difference in later life. This is evident if one looks at the
range of make-believe play shown by children in different nur-

sery schools and from different cultural backgrounds. Children who have very little make-believe in their repertory are likely to be handicapped as they move from their home into nursery or later school situations. They have not tried out different possibilities in advance. The role of the schoolchild is a very important new role a child must learn.

A very dramatic example of how fantasy plays a role in school preparation emerged in an important piece of research carried out by Dr. Sara Smilansky. She developed a series of games for three-year-olds which helped them make the transition to school much more smoothly and opened the way for more enjoyable and effective learning in kindergarten. A game such as Going to the Supermarket can be of great importance to the early preschooler in building toward the transition to roles that will be played outside the home. Imaginative games that involve moving through the aisles, choosing items, reading prices, paying at the checkout counter, bringing items home and preparing meals set up a series of structures and separate acts that help prepare a child for the formal arrangements of school. Playing school itself, often with the help of older children, can be tremendously valuable as well.

Once you have prepared your child more effectively to engage in sociodramatic games, you've opened a door to many additional ways of making contact with other children and learning further roles along the way. One of the most constructive features of nursery school and of free play in playgrounds or backyards is children's interaction around pretend games. The child who quickly grasps the terms of a "space trip" or a "picnic" moves smoothly into a small group. The children assign each other roles and often switch them, taking turns at being the "daddy" or the "good guy." A great deal of important learning takes place in these games, for the child not only hears of new roles, but also learns to accommodate to the demands of a game or to the ebb and flow of the mood of a small group.

Sociodramatic play of the type we are advocating has other important features beyond the introduction to social roles, of course. Children caught up in an interesting make-believe game are much less likely to become restless and to engage in direct physical conflict with each other. They are also acquiring skill in looking at situations from different points of view, for sometimes they are the "bad guys," sometimes their "victims." Observations of nursery play by Dr. Rosalind Gould led her to conclude that children who have learned to see the other children's point of view through make-believe are much less likely to become physically aggressive or vicious in their behavior.

Make-believe play provides other advantages. Psychotherapists regularly rely on the play of children with doll families to pick up signs of confusion or conflict in a disturbed child. A child who has been poorly prepared for early school experience may reveal this through a game in which "school" and "jail" get mixed up. Often the child who has failed to develop much skill at make-believe has difficulty expressing his conflicts to a therapist or becoming involved in the treatment. Dr. Joanne Fineman's experiences in play therapy indicate that children who came for treatment with little ability to engage in sociodramatic games did not make progress in overcoming their conflicts.

While you are not planning to carry out psychotherapy with your child, you can learn a great deal from watching his or her make-believe games. Consider the case of a child who is feeling very jealous of a new baby in the family. You may notice make-believe games at school or at home in which imaginary crying babies or dolls are always scolded or spanked, or suffer horrendous punishments. This suggests that the child wants more attention. It also opens the way for introducing other pretend play that will help an older sibling learn the *role* of being a big brother or sister. By introducing sociodramatic play that provides alternatives through caretaking and sharing, you can help the child gain a sense of self-esteem and handle his understandable annoyance at the newcomer in a more constructive fashion.

Once you have initiated make-believe, it is important to begin phasing yourself out and let the child carry on alone or with friends. Your job as an adult should be to set the scene and help to suggest a story line (possibly even one of the games you played in the preceding chapter, such as *Ping* or *Caps for Sale,* if the child prefers that to some real-life roles). You may be needed to provide props or simple costumes, hats, shoes, a vest or long dress, but once you have indicated to the child how he can be the teacher, doctor, carwasher, move away. It doesn't matter if the events are out of sequence or the facts inaccurate. Let him make believe in his own way with his own material and ideas. Your job is only to be there to help when asked, or to moderate a disagreement. One of the hidden assets you will find emerging from these games and exercises is an increase in sharing and taking turns.

ACTIVITY: **SOCIODRAMATIC PLAY**

1. School

MATERIALS

>Tables, chairs, books, papers, pencils, eraser, glue, paper clips, stapler, staples, rubber bands, crayons, felt-tip markers, rulers, clock (made from a paper plate), bell, Scotch tape, lunchbox for snack, gold stars, chalk, blackboard.

In general, four- and five-year-olds are more interested in playing school than two- and three-year-olds. Girls tend to initiate school more than boys, so you may want to try a switch and ask one of the boys to be the teacher. You can start off the game by showing the children some things to do at school.

Let's write numbers.
Let's write our ABC's.
Let's have story time.

Depending on the skills and age of your child or children, you can do the simplest school task (even scribbling) or more complex activities such as writing numbers and alphabet letters. You may start by ringing the bell, and saying: "School begins." Let the children sit in rows or in a circle and take turns being the teacher. They can also alternate going to the blackboard, giving out the paper, erasing the board.

Teacher can ring the bell for exercise and lead a "Simon Says" game.

Teacher can lead a song: "Old MacDonald Had a Farm."

There can be time out for snacks and time out for a book or record corner period.

You can be as elaborate as you wish in terms of activities. Simple arts and crafts work is fun for everyone. Put each child's name on his work and save it.

2. House Painter

This game is for the more adventuresome parent or teacher. It is probably best played in the backyard or the nursery school playground. We remember the children at Elmwood Nursery School in Westchester gleefully painting their playhouse. The game lasted for days and the paint color was changed with every new "house painter" who joined in the fun. Real paint was used, latex-based so it was washable, but plain water with food coloring is less expensive and may be preferred.

MATERIALS

Empty plastic ice cream or margarine containers for paint, water and food coloring, or latex paint; paint-brushes; visor or old cap; sticks for stirring paint; overalls, old blue jeans, or discarded shirts that serve as smocks;

small stepladder—preferably a two-step stool for reaching; a readily available sink or wash basin; water and paper towels for cleaning brushes; paint catalogues and sample paint chips; large appliance carton for the "house," "table," "garage" or whatever is to be painted; if shoe boxes or cereal boxes are used too, they can become "blocks" for building when they have dried.

Two children or more can play house painter, or even one child if you join in and play a role. Let the painter choose a name for himself and a name for the paint company. You can help set up a simple game such as the following:

Mrs. Smith: "Hello, this is Mrs. Smith. My house is all peeling and dirty. Would you come and bring your book of colors?"

The Painter: "I'll be over this afternoon with my samples."

The painter can visit Mr. or Mrs. Smith and bring his sample color chips or paint catalogue. (Here is a chance to practice some color memory.) Help the children make a choice among the colors that you have available. When the customer decides on the color, the painter can talk about price.

The best part is when the job begins. Mr. or Mrs. Smith can now switch roles and join in as the painter's helper or partner. Let the children mix the colors and experiment with the strokes. This kind of play needs an adult close by for supervision and to set the roles. As in the case of any water play, be prepared for some mess and minor skirmishes. The fun is worth the risk.

3. More Water Games

Janitor and Car Wash are good outdoor games, though we have played car wash indoors on a table with a washable surface, using toy cars, a wash basin and some rags. Blocks were used to form the car wash garage and plastic men were enlisted to help do the work. Outdoors, of course, you can do a splendid job of car wash with fewer prohibitions against spilling and general mess.

MATERIALS FOR JANITOR

> Mop, pails, sponges, broom, plastic squeeze bottles (leftover detergent bottles are fine), paper towels, squeegee, rags, apron, dustpans.

MATERIALS FOR CAR WASH

> Toy cars or trucks, bicycles, toy fire engines, rags, pail, squeegee, plastic squeeze bottles, boots or rubbers, garden hose (if you're willing), paper money.

Both games can be played with one child or more. Choose a child to play the role of janitor and one to be the lady or man of the house. If you do this out of doors, set up a small house made of boxes or garden furniture that can't be damaged by water. The children can sweep the walk, dust and wash the chairs, and pretend that the boxes are furniture and spray them with water.

In the car wash game, the children can line up on their "cars" and drive them into the car wash garage. You can help them set up the "garage" space in your driveway or backyard by placing long blocks, stacked on each other, in facing rows about one foot high, to allow the car to drive between them for the wash.

The car wash people should wear boots or rubbers unless it is a summer day, when bare feet are perfect. If you permit use of the hose, we suggest you take off the nozzle, so that the spray is more controlled.

Begin by letting one car at a time drive up to the garage. If you wish, make a sign out of cardboard and fasten it to the "garage door" or to a tree. The sign can have the name of the garage, the price per wash and the price of a waxing. Part of the fun is choosing a name for the car wash and deciding on the prices. Place a shoe box on a table for collecting the paper money.

As each child has his turn, you can help with the dialogue.

"Drive right up."

"Close all your windows."

"Leave the key in the car."

"Do you want regular wash or wax wash?"

The children can take turns playing car washers and drivers.

4. Restaurant

This game can be played indoors, and if weather permits and a yard is available, outdoors as well.

MATERIALS

> Tables and chairs; "order pad" made from pieces of paper stapled to cardboard; old menus, or menus you have made

with the children; play dishes, silverware, trays, center-pieces, made by the children out of flowers, clay animals, abstract sculptures; candles; paper doilies; aprons; plastic or paper place mats, paper napkins; simple snacks (finger food); sponge for cleanup; paper money.

Restaurant is a variation of Tea Party, which boys and girls can share, playing waiters and guests equally. The preparations are as much fun as the actual game. Four- and five-year-olds may enjoy this more than younger children.

Setting up the restaurant is the initial step. Give the children a corner of the kitchen, dining room, playroom, or if a backyard is available, use the picnic table. First work on the centerpieces. Here let the children be as imaginative as they wish, using paper flowers, a bowl of paper fruit, clay candles or animals, or abstract sculpture made from pipe cleaners with pieces of colored construction paper attached by Scotch tape.

Next prepare the order pads. Cut paper into 3' × 5' pieces and staple one end to a cardboard of the same size. Loop the pencil through a corner of the cardboard by a string long enough to permit writing down the order. Pretend writing is fine and should be encouraged.

Then set the table. The children can use toy dishes or paper plates and cups. Have the table fully set before the "customers" arrive. Offer them old menus or let the children make their own. Help with the spelling of words of things to eat, but let them decorate the menus by themselves. Paper pasted on a colored sheet of construction paper looks festive.

When all is ready, you can suggest procedures to the children or demonstrate them first—how customers arrive, hang up their coats, and then are shown to the table by the waiter. When the children order, let them choose anything they wish. As for food, raisins can be meat, water soup, cookies a fancy dessert, a cup of water or milk, tea or coffee. Show the "waiters" how to clear the table. The "waiter" presents the check to each "customer" when the meal is over and the customers should pay the cashier with play money.

5. Doctor, Nurse, Hospital

Children love to play doctor, perhaps because so very early in their lives the doctor is one of the first professionals, or people other than their parents, who are closely involved with their development. Playing doctor also eases some of the tensions and concerns children have about their own bodies, their fear of pain and inoculations, and their general curiosity about parts of the body. Most children can play doctor without too much help from you about how to proceed, but you can suggest ideas such as an eye test using a homemade chart, a sling, an ambulance made from a bike attached to a wagon by a sturdy cord, a chair to serve as a wheelchair, and the switching of roles so that both boys and girls play nurse and doctor.

MATERIALS

> Doctor's bag (a small overnight case); Band-Aids; empty, thoroughly washed pill bottles (with raisins for pills); small plastic bottle (with juice for medicine); splints; plastic syringes found in toy doctor kits; an old sheet cut up for slings and bandages; adhesive tape; stethoscope (toy ones are widely available); white shirt for uniform; nurses' caps made out of white construction paper and staples; draw a red cross on the front; eye chart (shirt cardboards on which the children draw numbers or designs with black crayons or felt-tip markers; help them make the figures smaller as you go down the chart); toy telephone for the receptionist; rubber stamp to use for paid bills; sofa or bench for examining table; paper for prescriptions; table, a chair and magazines in the "waiting room."

Start the game of doctor by arranging the "office" or "hospital." A small corner can be the reception room. Place the toy phone on a table and let one of the children be the receptionist nurse who first greets the "patient," with or without his "mommy." Show the nurse how to ask for the patient's name and how to call to the doctor to tell him the patient has arrived.

The doctor can then bring the patient into the examining room: a corner nearby with all the necessary materials arranged on a little table—Band-Aids, stethoscope, "pills"—and a sofa or bench that serves as the examining table. You can suggest a different series of ailments each time you play:

> eye trouble
> a broken arm (fun because it involves splint, bandages and sling)
> a tummyache (the remedy is a few raisin "pills")
> a bad cold (the remedy is cough medicine—juice in a small bottle)

The children can take turns playing doctor, nurse, patient, ambulance driver (outdoors, use the bike with a wagon attached; indoors, a large box makes a good ambulance). Once you have helped start the dialogue, you will find that the children take over and act out their own concerns or experiences with the doctor. As you listen in you are likely to learn something about their anxieties in regard to their own bodies.

ACTIVITY: **GAMES THAT REPRODUCE THE NEIGHBORHOOD**

The games that follow will help your child learn something about his neighborhood—the places he sees most often. They will help him understand the world around him, interact with other people, and deal with novel experiences. The routine act of going to the supermarket can become an engrossing game, and there are equally satisfying variations: the firehouse, the laundromat, the zoo, the police station, or a local farm if there is one nearby. Once you get the idea, your own imagination will lead the way.

1. Post Office

This is easy to play at home, with a minimum of mess. The child can "buy" a stamp. He learns that there are different prices for stamps; that bigger, fatter envelopes require more postage than thin ones; that letters sent out of the country are more expensive too. Let him lick the envelope and seal it, put the letter on the scale, and paste the stamps on the envelope, using a little sponge. The climax, of course, is dropping the mail in the slot.

MATERIALS

Shoulder bags; old envelopes; paper; junk mail; old magazines; old postcards; make-believe stamps that you let the children draw (any design they choose); old canceled stamps or Christmas or Easter seals; glue or paste; small scale; sponge and bowl of water; pens, pencils; stamp pad and rubber stamp; postman's hat and whistle (an old baseball hat with a paper patch stapled on front saying "U.S. Mail" is easy to make); slotted cardboard box to drop the letters in; paper money.

Set up a small post office, using as your table that all-purpose appliance box, the kitchen table or a card table. Place all your equipment on the box—stamps, rubber stamp, sponge and bowl of water, scale. Put shoe boxes inside for sorting the old postcards, magazines and junk mail which serve as the children's "mail."

One child is postman. The others come to buy stamps, mail letters and collect their mail. The postman—the children can take turns at this—stands behind the box or table and sells the stamps. Demonstrate:

buying a stamp
weighing a letter (if you have a scale)
pasting on the stamp

dropping the letter into a slit you've made in the large box

collecting mail from the postman

You can enlarge the game by playing delivery. Close up the post office. Each child goes to a "house"—a sofa, a big easy chair, a small corner of the room. The mailman places the letters in his bag, puts on his cap, blows his whistle and delivers the mail. Everyone gets mail, and everyone has a turn playing postman.

2. Shoe Store

Worn out or discarded shoes are the basic equipment for "shoe store." In the nursery school or day care center, the shoes in the dress-up corner will serve.

MATERIALS

Boxes or paper bags, shoes, boots, rubbers, chairs, sales pads (paper you have cut and stapled to cardboard), pencils, foot-long ruler, paper money.

Line up all the shoes on the floor in display fashion. Choose a child to be salesperson and begin by suggesting some starting dialogue:

"Hello, we need some shoes today."
"Let me measure your foot. You need size three."
"What kind of shoe do you like? What color?"
"This one is too tight [too big, just right]."

Show how salespeople wrap the shoes and customers pay for them. Make sure everyone takes turns.

3. Laundromat or Cleaners

MATERIALS

Laundry basket, empty plastic soap containers, old clothes, or clothes from the dress-up box, dishpan, clothespins, ironing board and iron, hangers, toy clock or kitchen timer, cash register, play money, large boxes labeled "washer" and "dryer."

Laundromat games have many practical benefits. They help children to separate colors (sorting dark and light clothes), match them (pairing socks), count items and improve dexterity (folding clothes). It also prepares them for the roles that boys and girls will share increasingly in the running of a household.

4. Grocery Store

MATERIALS

Boxes or long table for counters, boxes for shelves, empty cereal and cracker boxes, cans without sharp edges, soaps, cleaning supplies, paper goods, fruits and vegetables, signs for the different foods, toy cash register, play money, telephone, order pads and pencils, wagon for deliveries.

Playing grocer helps the four- and five-year-old to differentiate numbers and letters, sizes and shapes, and begin to read. Start the dialogue by being Mrs. Smith and giving your order. The grocer will fill it by selecting items and putting them in the wagon. You can even have a delivery boy bring them to Mrs. Smith. Let the children take turns playing the different roles— writing the orders, being the cashier, answering the telephone, acting as the customer.

5. Bakery

MATERIALS

INDOORS:

Play dough, cookie cutter, rolling pin, pastry containers such as tinfoil tart shells, cupcake pans or cupcake liners, decorations such as raisins, small birthday candles, colored sprinkles, small buttons.

OUTDOORS:

Sandbox, sieves, shovels, little trucks for delivery, decorations such as sticks, pebbles, shells, containers such as old cupcake pans, cookie cutters.

Bakery is a favorite game because it can easily be transfered outside to the sandbox. Here you will want a little water. Sand sieves, shovels and little trucks to deliver the cakes can add to the fun. One boy made marvelous mud cakes and decorated them with the white seeds of nearby dandelions. In the middle of the game, he decided suddenly to make snowballs instead and turned Bakery into a Snowball game. This kind of imaginative extension in play is worth encouraging.

6. Library

MATERIALS

Books, records, simple boxes for shelves (stacks of empty shoe boxes), table, rubber stamp and pad, pencils, library cards (made out of cardboard, or 3″ × 5″ index cards), chairs.

Children should be familiar with a library before playing this game so that they understand this special place. At home you can arrange the books and records on a table and let your child select the book he wants. Make him a library card by printing his name on the top of an index card. Make up a name for your library. Let your child play librarian and stamp a card for you as you pretend to borrow a book.

Rainy days are fun for library play. As a special treat you can provide the story hour by letting each child choose a short story for you to read. Encourage them to be the librarian in turn, and to tell the story as they turn the pages, pretending to read even if they can't.

ACTIVITY: **PEOPLE TO BE WHEN YOU'RE ALONE**

There are times when a child simply has no available companionship. Under these circumstances, children make increasing demands upon adults, and stress and impatience mount on both sides.

Some children—especially older or first-born youngsters—develop imaginary companions with whom they talk or play when there are no opportunities to play with contemporaries or with adults. Children born blind almost always have an imaginary playmate who is sighted.

If an imaginary companion lasts into adult life, as in the well-known play *Harvey,* whose hero takes his invisible full-sized rabbit to his favorite bar, the situation is likely to be pathological; but this is very rare and no available research indicates that imaginary companions in childhood are anything other than a normal form of make-believe.

Going to bed at night can be a frightening and lonely experience for the child between the ages of two and five. By this time children have developed a complex attachment to their parents and have also learned to use the familiar objects they see around them at home as navigational features. When the lights are turned off, this familiar environment becomes frightening and bewildering. The play of light and shadows on the wall, the noises from the street, are not easily identified. Many of the child's fantasies of bogey men or goblins grow from such experiences in the dark, aided all too often by teasing from older children, relatives and occasionally even parents. In these nightly bedtime crises, it is comforting indeed for the youngster to have a cuddly plush rabbit or teddy bear who can "talk" to him, or an imaginary friend who is even more afraid and so can be consoled.

Many children two to five years old are expected to take a daily nap. Often parents can hear them chattering in their rooms, manipulating toys or engaging in bits of make-believe to pass the time when they cannot fall asleep. The child who lacks sufficient resources or skill in fantasy play may find a naptime like this intolerable and become irritable or tearful.

The following games are to be played by a child when he is alone. Some of the preceding games, as noted, may also be adapted for a single child.

1. Newspaper Reporter

MATERIALS

Typewriter, toy telephone, desk, table (or old box), chair, toy camera (made from a small box), pens, pencils, old newspapers.

This game is likely to appeal to a five-year-old rather than a younger child. Show the child a newspaper and the kinds of material it contains, and explain why people read it. Describe the kinds of news items he might use to write a news story of his own, such as:

> something that happened at your house
> taking care of a pet (dog, cat, gerbils, goldfish)
> the birthday of a relative
> a new neighbor
> a make-believe fire in the neighborhood
> a lost dog

Help your child to write a story. Paste it on a large blank sheet of paper. He can illustrate the story himself, or search through magazines for pictures to paste next to his story. His "newspaper" can contain any poem he writes, any picture he draws, or any picture or advertisement he cuts out from old magazines or newspapers. Making up a name for the paper is fun; help him print it on top of his large sheet of blank paper before he begins.

2. Carpenter

MATERIALS

> Sandpaper, wood scraps with smooth edges, belt, toolbox (shoe box or flight bag), hammer, nails, pliers, screwdrivers, old hat and coveralls, worktable.

Most nursery schools have a "carpenter" corner. If you choose to set up an area for your child where he or she can use simple tools, be sure that this is a supervised activity and that he learns how to use a saw or hammer correctly. See that the wood scraps are sufficiently large so hammering doesn't lead to split wood and frustration. The four- or five-year-old likes to hammer and with your help can make a rudimentary airplane, bookends, a little box for treasures. He may simply like to hammer nails into wood just for the act of mastery and not need to make anything at all!

3. Camper

MATERIALS

Knapsack or flight bag, canteen or Thermos, plastic dishes, fishing pole, long-handled strainer for catching fish, frying pan, toy shovel, sleeping bag, flashlight, sticks for fire, snack for food.

You can help your camper by pretending you are looking for a quiet place in the woods near a make-believe river or stream. Show him how to rub sticks together for a "fire." Put the frying pan over it to cook an imaginary steak. Catch a fish or two. Sing some songs by the "campfire" and roll into the sleeping bag for a snug night's sleep.

4. Gardener

MATERIALS

Set of plastic garden tools or sticks that can serve as make-believe tools, pail, watering can, hose (your vacuum attachment) for make-believe water, empty seed packets, fake flowers (construction paper and pipe cleaners or play dough).

The child can play make-believe garden or real garden. In the pretend garden, the living room rug can be grass, and a plastic shovel used to "dig." The child pretends to plant a seed, water it, watch it grow—pick it, smell it (flowers made from paper can be "planted" on the rug and later put in a vase). The real garden is a small window box. Growing vegetables from a potato or carrot is fairly easy, or the child can plant flower seeds and watch them grow. The real garden takes time and the child should be reminded of this. The make-believe garden can be a source of immediate pleasure by following the growing stages in the imagination, and making the flowers. Both games can be played simultaneously and the child will learn to tend his real garden through his rehearsal in make-believe. The delay of waiting to pick his real flower can be eased through the make-believe play.

ACTIVITY: **ADVENTURE GAMES—SOME PEOPLE TO BE WHEN THERE ARE MORE THAN ONE**

Children also need to run and whoop and holler. This may be hard on adults indoors, but the pleasure youngsters take in a good adventure game—pirates, cowboys and Indians, Robin Hood, wild animals—is worth it.

1. Pirates

MATERIALS

Scarves, black patches, mustache (cut from black construction paper), boots, treasure box and treasure (play dough gold), ocean (blue crepe paper or felt), island, shovels, maps, daggers (made out of cardboard), ship, sharks.

Indoors, Pirates can be played on a card table, using blue crepe paper for the ocean, pipe cleaners for pirates, play dough for islands and sharks, and small blocks to represent ships.

The ships can be made to sail along until the island is sighted. Suggest adventures on the way: man overboard, sharks coming, storm, rescue at sea and the grand finale (accompanied by a chorus of "Ho, ho, ho, and a bottle of rum"), when previously hidden treasures (snacks tucked away by the adult before the game began) are uncovered.

Outdoors, you can be freer with space. Let the children actually dig for treasure which you have hidden under a pile of leaves beforehand. Boxes can be the boats and some of the children can be the sharks or whales.

2. Cowboys and Indians

Children need very little help in learning how to play this game. They imitate older children on the block, as well as television shows. You can help play the game indoors with plastic toys and a block fort. You won't need to participate very long. Indoors and out, the main themes are the attack, the chase, the big fight, the rescue, fallen bodies.

Children can learn something about how Indians lived by being read books that describe their housing, customs, crafts and skills. When they play cowboy and Indian, you can help them make a small Indian village, constructing a tepee, a paper canoe, and a totem pole, based on pictures in books. The cowboy and Indian "fight" game can be varied to include a peaceful cowboy and Indian meeting, smoking a peace pipe, or having an Indian and cowboy contest, consisting of horseback riding, roping, and hunting.

3. Firemen

MATERIALS

Fireman's hat (made out of red construction paper), fire engine (boxes turned upside down), blocks (wooden or plastic), small bell or two spoons tied together, hose (vacuum cleaner hose or one made from two cardboard paper towel cylinders taped together), small cars to use as fire engines.

You can start the game by ringing a bell and yelling, "Fire!" The child can put on his hat, take his "engine" out of a "block" firehouse and race to put out the fire. Build a little house or school or factory out of blocks and show the child how to rescue the people. Put plastic figures in the "windows" to make the buildings look real. If you play outdoors, large boxes become the fire engines and boulders or trees the buildings that are on fire.

Going to Bed or Naptime

Earlier in this chapter, we talked about the difficulties some children experience concerning bedtime and naptime. They may need a night light, a special toy in their bed, a ritual glass of water, story or kiss before they go to sleep. This is normal behavior and as the child grows he eventually relinquishes such nighttime props. Some children take longer than others to finally accept bedtime as a routine part of life, and they may need some help.

We suggest a simple story or song that the child chooses. You can also make up a continuing story that has a new chapter each nap or bedtime. Playing a soothing record (see Appendix A) may help too. Try not to prolong this period before bedtime, however, or you will find yourself involved in an hour of unending rituals.

We also suggest telling your child to imagine a happy thing and think about it before he goes to sleep. A birthday party, a trip to the zoo, a playmate he likes, are concrete experiences that a child can relieve in his mind's eye, relaxing him so that he falls asleep.

7

Special Ways for Special Days

For the preschooler, who has as yet little experience in different settings both inside and outside the home, there are dozens of situations that seem strange, confusing, boring or threatening. Make-believe games can help a child cope with these troublesome times or settings because the play situation provides an *alternative* environment which is almost completely under the child's control. The games described in this chapter are designed to help a child develop a repertory of diversions or techniques that can be drawn upon in those periods of restlessness, threat or stress which all youngsters must inevitably confront. Waiting in itself is difficult for some children; the confusion of sights and sounds in a supermarket can be stressful for others. In a dentist's or doctor's office, fear added to restlessness can make for a difficult time. Bathtime is scary for some children. Simply going off to sleep at night in a darkened room poses difficulties for all very young children at one time or another. Then, of course, there are those sick-in-bed days when not only does the tummy hurt but the hours drag on in the isolation of the bedroom. Here, then, are some ways that imagination can provide a new, child-controllable environment for difficult hours or days.

ACTIVITY: **WAITING TIME**

All of us, children and adults alike, find ourselves in many situations that require sitting quietly and waiting until the doctor, the dentist or the government clerk calls us in for our appointment. There are waits for trains or buses. There are long, dull nighttime car rides with little to do to pass the time. Circumstances like these are particularly trying for children. They squirm and fuss. Young children lack the adult faculty for reading or losing themselves in thought. A preschooler is likely to be physically active, to move around, exploring the environment. If he finds the bus terminal waiting room boring, he may pull at some of the posters on the wall or collect the timetables set neatly on the counter and make his own private pile, annoying the clerk. The child with skill at make-believe, who has one or two small, simple toys, a couple of interesting-looking sticks, perhaps a plastic cowboy or Indian figure, or a few miniature cars, can quickly generate an elaborate game that minimizes the likelihood of clashes with adults.

The old saying that "children should be seen and not heard" sometimes reflects a necessary reality. The child with resources for entertaining himself under these circumstances is less likely to become involved in repeated scoldings or the physical expression of adult displeasure. The extremely active child who is constantly touching and examining and exploring is very likely to find himself labeled bothersome or "bad." This can foster negative self-concepts that make for problems in later life.

How can you make a trip to the doctor, dentist, airport or bus terminal more pleasant for you and your child? We will suggest some games and ideas to use in a waiting situation. In the preceding chapter we talked about sociodramatic play and suggested doctor and airplane games. Certainly you can include dentist, bus driver and other roles as you see fit. Playing doctor or dentist with your child before a visit can be the initial step for those of you whose children start to balk even *before* they get to the waiting room. Role playing, remember, helps the child assimilate information about what the doctor, nurse or pilot does, and acting out the role helps the child master some of his concerns and fears about the strange situation.

It is a simple and helpful technique to keep a small box or bag of special toys or games that you can take along when you are going to be caught in a waiting period with your child. The toys and games should be relatively simple, small and adaptable. Small plastic figures of animals, cowboys, Indians, pirates and family members are good to have. Include small cars, small blocks and some simple craft materials that will not require cleanup, such as pipe cleaners, play dough and bottle caps. We also suggest taking crayons, coloring books or pads, and storybooks that haven't been read before. Tell the child this is his special Waiting Time Bag, to be used only for those outings that you know will require your child to amuse himself. Long automobile trips and airplane flights, as well as waiting rooms, will be much more pleasant.

Many pediatricians and pediatric dentists have special toy boxes for children. Don't count on them, however. The toys are often in bad repair, have missing parts or pieces, and are generally fought over by the youngsters in the room.

1. Toy Bag Games

Help your child set up a garage, fort or house with small blocks (Lego blocks are ideal), and use the appropriate small toy figures to play each game.

MATERIALS

FERRY BOAT: Small plastic boats or blocks; blue felt or oilcloth for the water; small plastic people (or pipe cleaners, wooden clothespins, etc.) for passengers; make-believe sounds of ferry whistle, bell, wind.

PARKING LOT: Small cars; trucks; small blocks made into booth for tickets, and for columns, floors and elevator; miniature figures for drivers and attendant.

KING AND QUEEN: Small castle made of blocks; miniature figures of people; miniature dinosaurs, or figures made from pipe cleaners or play dough, to be dragons and a wicked witch; plastic knights and horses.

SPACE TRIP: Small toy rocket ship; blocks to build a house on a planet; miniature people to fly on the rocket ship and to live on the planet; play dough or clay for food, animals, scenery on the planet.

STABLE: Small blocks for stalls; miniature horses; crumpled paper for hay; miniature figures to represent riders, stable hands, groom, riding instructor.

HOTEL: Small blocks for front desk, elevator; miniature figures to represent bellhops, desk clerk, guests, waiter; plants and lobby signs made from colored paper.

You can help the child with simple plots and dialogue for each situation; how much help will depend on his experience: these days most children have taken trips, been to hotels or motels, or seen stables on television shows. All these games are replays in miniature of our sociodramatic games. Once the youngster is started, he is likely to be able to continue by himself.

2. Games That Do Not Require Props

EXPLORER: All children like to explore. If your child knows the various colors, ask him or her to find something in the room that is blue, red, green, black, etc. You can make the game more complex by combining two concepts, such as color and shape or color and size: for example, find something small and red, or round and blue. This is a bit more difficult, but more of a challenge for the four- and five-year-old.

WORD GAMES: Word games can be played with five-year-olds and those four-year-olds who love words. Keeping score for you and your players motivates them.

> *Rhyming.* Give me a word that rhymes with red/sit/shoe.
> *Beginning.* Give me a word that starts with *h* as in "hole"/
> *d* as in "door"/*c* as in "cat."
> *Opposites.* Let your child fill in the missing opposite word:
>
> > If I'm not small, I'm . . .
> > If I'm not cold, I'm . . .
> > If I'm not happy, I'm . . .

> *Long Words—Short Words.* Have your child think of a long word, such as kangaroo/umbrella/locomotive/rubber band. Or think of a short word—they're easy: can/do/-big/bug.
>
> *Flower Words That Are Animals and Things.* This is hard, even for a five-year-old. Do it only if he can: dandelion/pussy willow/lady slipper/bachelor button/tiger lily.

CAR GAMES:

> *Looking for the License Plate.* Have the children spot a license plate that is from out of state—the color will be the clue since the words will be too hard. You can carry this a step further by suggesting that the children imagine who the people in each car are, where they are going, and what they will do when they get there.
>
> *Colorful Cars.* Choose a color; first child to see a car that color wins.
>
> *Animal Passengers.* Each child who sees a dog or cat in a passing car gets points. This is especially good in summer, when the roads are full of crowded vacationers' cars.

Tag-alongs. Each child who spots an attachment hooked onto a car (U-Haul, boat, trailer) gets a point.

Reading Game. This can be played with your child on a long trip if he or she is beginning to read. Have him look for signs that say: Stop/Food/Exit/Detour/Gasoline/Restaurant/Information/Toll Station, etc. You might try to play an alphabet game by having him search for a sign beginning with *A,* and then following consecutively down the alphabet. On a long trip this is a satisfying game.

SONGS:

The child sings a song using "la, la, la" instead of words. You guess the title from the tune.

The adult sings a song, leaving out a word, which the child can fill in: e.g., "Old MacDonald had a . . ."

Singing rounds: "Row, Row, Row Your Boat," "Frère Jacques," etc. Another song children love is "Eentsy Weentsy Spider":

Eentsy weentsy spider went up the waterspout.
Down came the rain and washed the spider out.
Out came the sun and dried up all the rain.
So the eentsy weentsy spider went up the spout again.

Improvised hand movements up and down for spider, rain and sun are simple and fun. "I'm a Little Teapot" is another song children enjoy, imitating the hand movements.

GUESS THE SOUND: Make sounds of trains, snap your fingers, imitate a horn, bell or the sounds of animals: owl/cow/horse/sheep/dog/cat. Have the child guess the object or animal.

GUESS WHAT I'M DRAWING: Take a pad and pencil and draw simple objects for the child to identify: cup/ice cream cone/train/cat/house/hand.

Start a Person/Object. You draw one part, then the child takes a turn. If you draw a round circle for a face, he can put in eyes, then you the nose and he the mouth. Let the child be free to do as he wants to as you continue the figure or object, such as a boat, a whale, a train, a clown, a dog or a rocket ship.

IMAGINE YOU ARE SOMEPLACE: You don't need any materials for this game. (Books that deal with imagination and games are suggested in Appendix A.) Start by saying: "Make believe I'm in the dime store. Here's what I see." Name the objects or describe everything about the scene. Then ask the child: "Make believe you're at the beach/at a party/at the zoo/in a submarine/in your bedroom/in the kitchen."

ACTIVITIES: **OUTINGS**

1. Supermarket Shopping

The routine trip to the supermarket can be an ordeal on days when a youngster feels out of sorts. We have all heard mothers exasperated by the cookie boxes that the wandering four-year-old has opened, the cereal boxes he has tossed into the shopping cart, or the money he wants for the gum machine. We have encountered toddlers crying "Mommy" or have seen them scurrying frantically around the aisles, "lost" and terrified. On days when nothing seems to please or direct your youngster, you may want to try some imaginative techniques.

If your three-year-old still fits in the front compartment of your cart, let him sit there and be the trainman. If he is too big, he can walk next to you pretending to be the trainman. Let him share the "driving" of the cart with you. He can even wear his trainman's hat on these trips. He starts the engine and away you go down the aisles. Let him know that you need to stop at each "city" to load up your supplies. If he's tall enough, he can help reach for items. You will have to enter into the spirit of the game if it is to work. Lots of praise as reinforcement keeps the game going. Be inventive: the frozen foods area is the North Pole; the fruits and vegetables are in the jungle; watch out for wild animals or other trains (shopping carts). Chinese food gets us to China, and the red sauces and macaroni find us in Italy. Checkout time is the last stop and your helper can unload the train with you.

2. Bank

When you have to go to the bank, suggest that your child bring some pennies. You can help him wrap them in a penny wrapper, and then give them to the teller for his own bank deposit or to exchange for coins of a larger denomination. Chances are that if your child enters into a transaction as he sees you do, he will be more eager to go, and better behaved. His own receipt or money envelope makes him feel important and more patient about your errands.

3. Department Store

A small tote bag for your child to carry for his own little packages will enable him to share the shopping experience. The escalator ride is exciting if you make believe it is "magic stairs." Try to shop early, when the store is least crowded. Lunch out in the store is a treat. Bring along simple snacks to help the morning seem less long for a child. Raisins, carrots, celery are not messy and will not interfere with appetites. If you have to try on clothes for yourself, bring along a coloring book or miniature toys so that your boy or girl can play in a corner while you are occupied. We once saw two little girls with Barbie dolls playing "shopping" by trying on Barbie outfits while their mother was buying her own dress.

ACTIVITIES: **INDOOR OCCASIONS**

1. Meals

Mealtime can be a contentious and strained experience for a child, especially if he's a picky eater and you're a worrier of a parent. You can relieve the *occasional* difficult feeding time with make-believe, though you should not allow this to develop into a ritual. As a general principle, start with very small portions if your children are fussy. The child can make believe he's a bird or a dog or a wild animal as he eats; the food will go down much more easily. The adult must be in a playful mood if this is to work. If the child still resists the food, don't force.

A doll or favorite animal "eating" along with the child is also fun. Putting a bib on the toy and giving it a special spoon and plate pleases the child and allows him to participate in giving the food to someone else so that he's in control.

A story at mealtime is often relaxing. Sometimes a child becomes so engrossed in the story—especially if you act out all the voices and sounds—that he doesn't even realize he's eating. A favorite record saved for mealtime also helps make this a pleasanter occasion. So does casual conversation about the day's events. The important thing is to keep eating times stress-free and relaxed, and not to worry unduly about occasional eating problems.

2. Bath

Most children love taking baths. But occasionally soap in the eyes or water that's too hot or too cold can turn them away temporarily. Floating rubber toys, fish, little boats or balls can make bathtime more enjoyable. Washing a doll, including its hair, allows the child to see this as fun, and be less resistant to having his own hair washed. The game of fishing—trying to catch a plastic or rubber fish—or "storm"—paddling along and then whipping up the water—are all helpful in making bath-time less fearful. Children will enjoy a playtime in the bathtub after they are soaped and rinsed. Songs like "Row, Row, Row Your Boat" are suitable for bathtime too.

3. Sick in Bed

When your child is really ill, sleep and rest are the main things he needs and wants. The games below are directed toward the recovery period, when he must remain in bed but is lively enough to require diversion.

Many of the color and word games described earlier in this chapter are suitable for playing in bed. Drawing pads, crayons and colored pencils, and coloring books are of course essential. Some children like to put simple puzzles together, and you can find numerous books suggesting arts and crafts for the bedridden child. There are also a variety of make-believe games that can be played in bed. A bed tray is very helpful if you have one, because the hard surface will enable the child to play with his toys without their falling over or getting lost in the bedclothes.

VARIATIONS

PIRATES: The pirate game is adaptable for the bed tray. Make an ocean out of blue crepe paper or construction paper. Use play dough to make an island, with smaller pieces of clay for the fish, the boats and even the sailors. You may also use miniature boats if you have them, or small blocks. Improvise the pirate game we described earlier and help your child play it.

CIRCUS: A circus will always cheer up a sick child. Again use the bed tray. The circus rings can be small loops from a ring toss game or wooden embroidery rings if you have them. If none of these is available, fashion rings out of pipe cleaners. You need miniature animals, a wild man, the fat lady, clowns, the trapeze artist, a tightrope walker. You can make your side-show figures out of clay and pipe cleaners. Signs and decorations can be fashioned from construction paper and felt-tip markers can be used for the lettering and drawings. Help your child make a tightrope; a simple device is a plastic straw resting on blocks placed several inches apart (Lego blocks are small enough for a bed tray) and held in place by pieces of play dough or clay. A trapeze can be a cut-open rubber band, with each end anchored with clay to its own block tower.

DOCTOR AND NURSE: A sick child likes to play doctor or nurse, and can play this with your assistance while he's in bed. You can easily adapt the ideas from Chapter 6 and use dolls or stuffed animals as the patients.

PUPPETS: A sickbed puppet show can be a source of amusement for your youngster, and other members of the family can be the audience. You can make a stage out of a small carton or a shoe box set on its side and placed on the bed tray. Use hand or finger puppets. Favorite fairy tales or nursery rhymes can offer story lines. Encourage your child to make up stories and use different voices. Help construct simple props out of paper,

blocks and small plastic containers. Little trees or bushes can be made out of clay. Tables and chairs for the puppets are built out of very small blocks or boxes, pieces of scrap material become curtains, tablecloths, scarves, a cape. The fun of making the puppets and scenery is a major part of the game and helps the time go by.

SENSORY GAMES: In the earlier chapters we talked about things to touch, see, taste, smell and hear, and these exercises can be adapted for your little patient: things to touch, hidden in the sock bag; things to smell. Be wary about tasting things unless the doctor says it's all right. You can prepare new things each day for touching, smelling, hearing, etc.

RECORDS AND MUSIC: You will want to use your record player while your child is recovering. We suggest you use the songs listed in Appendix A that allow both of you to play some make-believe games. Set up the record player near the child's bed, within his reach. You may also want to use a radio, trying to find programs that have music for children. If you use records, you and your child can sing along, and follow suggestions for simple hand movements or voice sound effects such as a squeaky door, a car skidding, machine noises or animals. Some records also suggest imaginative stories inspired by the music, such as an expedition to the moon, or a visit with a mad scientist, or a trip to a haunted house. Help your child to picture these scenes by trying to describe them and eliciting descriptions from him. You need no props; only the music.

STORIES: You will want to read to your youngster often when he is ill. If you both act out parts and take on the voices of characters, you will find reading with your child offers mutual pleasure. We have listed books in Appendix A according to topics. You can choose your stories to coincide with the game you play that day, such as a circus story to go with a circus game. Select stories that are funny or soothing, not too scary. Remember that when there is illness, there is bound to be some regression, so your child will seem more helpless than usual, and more dependent on you. He will probably want his favorite tales read and reread to him. He will also want you to be near him much of the time. He may be eager to hear books about going to the doctor. If his illness necessitates a hospital stay, you can prepare him by reading books about going to the hospital, as listed in Appendix A.

4. Birthday Parties

Many parents dread giving birthday parties for toddlers and preschoolers. The secret of a good party for your children is to keep it small. If you are trapped into having to include everyone and end up with twenty children, make sure enough adults are on hand to help out.

Birthday parties at this age should be short, no longer than an hour and a half at the most. This allows time for greetings, a few games, ice cream and cake, opening of presents and goodbyes, before excitement, too many children and a touch of jealousy make tempers flare.

We do not suggest competitive games for preschoolers. At this age, they are not very good losers, and party time is not the time to set up a win-lose situation. Parties generate excitement and tension to begin with, and the visiting children are inevitably envious of the party child. For this reason, a simple favor that each guest can take home as a souvenir is a good idea.

Before the day of the party, arrange to have small bags with twisters to hold the favors, candies, hat, horn or other goodies that each child will take home. The birthday child will enjoy helping with the party preparations. Let him or her choose the theme, colors for paper goods and candles, the hats and favors. Keep the cake a surprise, though.

GAMES: In addition to the suggestions listed below, you can play some of the games described in Chapter 4. Mr. Magician seems especially appropriate for a birthday party.

GUESS WHAT I SAID: The children sit in a circle and each one whispers a word or message to the child on his left, who passes it along in turn, and so on around the circle. The last child usually has a garbled sentence to repeat, much to everyone's delight.

MAKE A PARTY HAT: Have a large box filled with odds and ends—buttons, paper, ribbons, wood, scraps of material, pipe cleaners, etc. Help each child make a party hat. The frame can be construction paper taped or stapled together to fit the head size. Let the children cut, draw, or paste their own decorations on their hat.

TELL A STORY: You begin the story, and ask each child to add some event to it. This works well with four- and five-year-olds. If you tape-record it, the children love to hear it played back.

RHYTHM AND DANCE GAMES: If you play some of the records listed in Appendix A, the children can dance or move to the music as the song suggests. Children like this, and it allows them to let off some steam.

GUESS WHAT: Fill a big bag with distinctively-textured objects, and let each child close his eyes, reach in and feel an item. He has to tell you what it is without peeking.

PIN-ON GAMES: You can play variations on the pin-the-tail-on-the-donkey game, such as pin-a-nose-on-the-clown. This clown can be drawn simply with felt-tip markers on a large piece of oaktag. Noses can be big circles cut out of construction paper, with a different color for each child (write the child's name on the back of his paper nose). Your child may have his own idea for a pin-on game, and you can encourage him to help draw it.

A PUPPET BIRTHDAY PARTY: Using the puppet stage and puppets suggested in Chapter 5, you can help the children put on a simple play called "Birthday Party." Each child can have a puppet on his hand and one by one come to the party on the stage. A small cupcake with a candle can be the birthday cake, and everyone can sing "Happy Birthday."

THE SEARCH: Hide inexpensive favors around the room and allow the children, one by one, to search for them. You can play "hot and cold" and call out the appropriate signal to the child according to his distance from the hiding places.

The games and ideas presented here are by no means an exhaustive list. They are merely aids to help you develop your own routines and formulas for learning how to make any situation, even one as mundane as shopping or riding in a car, a more satisfying imaginative experience for your child. The active participation of children in routine activities, and in planning for special events such as a party, encourages them to develop resourcefulness and a more constructive attitude. The realm of make-believe enhances each experience, relieves boredom and frustration, and challenges your resourcefulness as a parent or teacher.

8

A Place for Fantasy and Make-Believe: Toys and Materials for Imaginative Play

If you are to encourage children to engage in the games and exercises in this book, you will want to plan an area or room that can become a special place for make-believe. Depending upon your resources—financial as well as spatial—this can be a corner of your child's bedroom or an entire playroom. If you are a teacher, you may want to consider rearranging your existing rooms to enable you to carry out some of the games.

Storage

It is essential to provide adequate storage for toys. If a child's play people are scattered throughout the house and blocks are dumped into a toy chest full of dress-up clothes, dolls, dishes, animals and trucks, the child will resist digging out what he needs, and may abandon a game before he starts. Empty coffee and cookie tins make good containers for miniatures; a shelf or area of a room can be set aside as a "parking lot"; shopping bags or an extra drawer make roomy containers for dress-up or doll clothes; cartons of various sizes can store construction toys. More elaborate and permanent storage equipment is, of course, sold everywhere. The point is that toys of a particular type must be stored together if they are to be accessible to the young child with minimal searching. When storage space is limited, one solution is periodically to put various toys out of sight, produce near-forgotten ones from attic, closet or cellar, and honor requests for the items removed when appropriate. The blocks that find their way into a bedroom to be used as tables in a doll house or fences for a farm will rarely be missed from the set; overall order is important for a child, not perfection.

Sturdiness

Sturdiness is a basic consideration. Children's toys are their possessions. It is misery to have a birthday present fail to perform as it should or break while the child is discovering what it is all about. Particularly disappointing for children are elaborate battery-driven toys that quickly break down.

Often household items make acceptable or superior substitutes for specific toys. Plastic containers make good spray bottles for a car wash game; measuring spoons are fun in the house corner; coffeepots are intriguing puzzles to two- and three-year-olds; plastic half-gallon bleach containers make good piggy banks when painted; wooden clothespins are good make-believe people; frozen juice cans are sturdy crayon containers.

BASIC MATERIALS IN YOUR FANTASY ROOM

Large Table	For drawing, painting, clay work and water play; small block-building; farms, pirate games, use of miniature toys; carpentry work; tea parties, restaurant; examining table for doctor. Table should be low and sturdy and have a washable surface.
Open Shelves	For blocks; small trucks; books; records and record player; shoe boxes, empty coffee, frozen

juice and cookie tins for paint and supplies, crayons, miniature toys, scissors, hole puncher, cellophane tape; band instruments. Divide the shelves so that they are separate units for each kind of item stored. Keep blocks separate from trucks and miniature toys to avoid clutter, and so that the children can see exactly what they want to play with. Colorful cushions on top of a low, wide shelf, which is securely fastened to the wall or storage unit, make a cozy place for sitting while reading or listening to records. If you do plan on seating space, this shelf should be approximately two feet above the floor and long enough for stretching out.

Dress-Up Corner   Small wall mirror; box for scarves, shoes, hats, pants and dresses; makeup, masks, jewelry.

Hideout or Nesting Place   A corner of a room that has some large open boxes turned on their sides, with ends tucked inside, for caves, igloos, forts, tents, etc. These boxes can also be store, house, post office or puppet stage area. The smaller boxes, such as shoe boxes, are the trains, cars, trucks.

Rooftop Hideaway   Climbing on a low stool or two-step ladder to reach a place high up is fun for any child. If you can build a sturdy lean-to, place a shag rug on top; the child will delight in climbing up to look down at everyone. This rooftop hideaway can lend itself to all sorts of games and adventures, and in playing house the child can make believe that his friend lives upstairs.

One way to make a rooftop hideaway is to use a large appliance box such as one that comes with a refrigerator. This can be painted with latex paints. If ends are tucked in, it is sturdy enough for a three- or four-year-old. You can turn it on its side or stand it upright. Smaller boxes placed inside the larger one reinforce it. Cartons that held tissue boxes can fit into the large appliance box. If you are handy with tools you can make a more elaborate construction, mounting a piece of plywood 4' × 4' on two sawhorses, 3' × 3', placed at either end for support. Another hideaway can be made with a sturdy card table covered by a long felt cloth. Children like to crawl under things and hide. The cloth can easily be fastened to the front legs of the table to make a curtainlike "door." The area inside can become a cozy cave, dollhouse, clubhouse, store or even a storage area.

If you set your hideaway in a corner of the room, two sides are there already.

Paint Corner   Easel standing on oilcloth or plastic drop cloth, blackboard, chalk, erasers, paints, brushes, rags for cleaning spills, plastic basin with water for cleaning brushes, supply of paper. Supplies should be kept on the storage shelves.

Watering Place   If you have a sink in your classroom or in an adjacent bathroom at home, have a stepstool nearby, with dispensers for paper towels and paper cups, and a small plastic basin.

If there is no sink, for games such as Pirates and car wash use a small basin partially filled with water and place it on the worktable with a plastic cloth underneath the table and the basin.

Science and   Shelf on which to keep plants, rock collections,
Animals   nests, dried leaves, berries and a magnifying lens. This shelf will be helpful to have when you work on the sense modalities—sight, touch, smell. Keep items for these sensory exercises on the shelf, and replenish them often. Each time you take a walk outside, encourage your child to find

a new rock to touch, a new flower to smell, a new object to feel, such as a feather, a piece of bark or a pine needle.

Animals like gerbils, hamsters or white mice are marvelous in the schoolroom. You can easily have animals such as these at home too. Let the children learn to feed them and help clean the cages. The animal in the cage can be used in puppet shows to change into the hand puppet prince or princess, and after the transformation the cage can be moved off the puppet stage and out of sight. A goldfish in a small bowl is a wonderful prop for a pirate game.

Household Corner   Shelf for toy cups, spoons, pots; cardboard boxes to serve as a stove and refrigerator. Dolls, doll clothes, doll carriages, beds (a shoe box can be a bed or doll's crib). Use the worktable, as noted, for tea parties and restaurant games. Have housecleaning supplies such as a small broom, dustpan and dustcloths available in this corner.

Movable Wall   A piece of wallboard about 4' × 4' framed by a molding and mounted on casters enables your child to make an instant room. He can divide his play area in any manner by moving his "wall." In a classroom, several of these dividers are ideal, but even a single one in a playroom gives a child privacy, as well as serving in a game when he wants a divider between the restaurant kitchen and dining room, the doctor's office and waiting room, the king's chamber and the dragon's lair.

The pages that follow describe in greater detail some of the toys you can use in the fantasy room. Some are homemade; others must be bought. A few toys in each category are all you need to get started. The games described in earlier chapters use

such materials in a variety of ways. Thus our emphasis is on the versatility of the materials as well as on their durability.

Indoor Equipment

One of the great thrills of childhood is to open a package and find a new toy. One of the joys of being a parent or teacher is to watch the delight of a child exploring the play possibilities of a new game or set of miniature cars, dolls or soldiers. While memory images and the examples of parents or teachers are often enough to stimulate make-believe play in children, there is little question that toys are especially exciting to preschoolers. For a two-year-old child a toy that has a specific function stimulates pretend play especially well. As children get older and have a richer store of images to draw on, the highly specific toy —the Barbie doll in bridal costume or preformed play dough— is likely to be less interesting over a period of time than relatively "unstructured" toys or playthings.

The section that follows is by no means a definitive list of what children should or will play with. It is a compilation of certain kinds of toys and materials which youngsters enjoy and which tend to stimulate make-believe play. Obviously, not all toys lead to make-believe play. Although a child may assemble a jigsaw puzzle and then slip into the realm of fantasy as he pretends its subject matter is real, puzzles are mainly mastery toys and pretend play is much more than mastery play. These toys have a useful function, but our emphasis is on other aspects of play.

Exploration may sometimes precede make-believe. A child must be familiar with the physical properties of blocks, water or sand in order to elaborate their use as tools. And the more ways in which he *can* use an item, the more ways he *will* use it. Thus flexibility has been a major criterion in assembling the selection that follows.

1. Real-Life Toys

There are three justifications for using a structured approach to pretend play: children love using the real thing; a box of objects suggestive of a specific game may help direct the child on a rainy day; and the possession of tools of a trade may help an excluded child join others in a complementary role or have his own play attract other children.

Objects from the kitchen such as an eggbeater, pots, aprons and strainers make useful "toys" in playing house. Daddy's tools, such as screwdrivers, hammers (used only under supervision), rulers, small wrenches and sandpaper, are fun to use for playing carpenter.

In sum, anything that is safe and fun goes. Children are forever using objects designed for one purpose for an entirely different one. This is pretend play at its best. Use your imagination and let the child use his.

2. Building Things

BLOCKS: Probably the most versatile indoor toys are kindergarten blocks. They are marketed in a wide range of prices, depending upon the hardness of the wood, the size and number of blocks and the variety of shapes in the set, and the cost of the container they come in. Once the child has mastered the structural properties of the blocks, he will go on to create whatever his fancy chooses. Blocks readily construct a farm, a dollhouse, a skyscraper, a zoo, a network of roads, a fire station, an entire village. Their possibilities are limited only by the number available, the imagination of the child, and his manipulative skill. Be sure to include some of the larger blocks in your set, and those shaped like wedges, arches, tunnels and cylinders.

Accessories can help block play come to life. Play people and animals made out of wood, rubber or plastic can be assigned roles and personalities. Miniature cowboys can reside in block ranches; soldiers can man their forts; spacemen their rocket ships. Cars, trucks and airplanes can move among block gas stations, garages, airports. Cardboard tubes, stones and shells can adorn structures in place of smokestacks, cannons and sculptures. Bits of fabric, paper and styrofoam can form tents, balconies, trees. Spools, sticks, buttons, cubes—the possibilities are endless, and once in the habit of improvising what he needs, the child will usually think of a substance that is suitable. Our experience has been that a set of top-quality blocks will remain in continuous use in a family or a nursery school, eagerly used by successive generations of children.

OTHER INDOOR CONSTRUCTION TOYS: Blocks are basic. Their qualities and potential for imaginative play have stimulated the creation of variations appropriate to the abilities and interests of young children. Colorful plastic bricks or logs that interlock have the advantage of rigidity and mobility. The maze of animal cages or fleet of ambulances which the child constructs with these cannot be easily destroyed by a baby brother who is learning to crawl or a "Batman" who sweeps through the room. Since the components are small, hundreds can be slipped into a small cardboard box when the family goes on vacation or the child faces a long wait for the dentist. Again, the addition of a few miniature people or cars can extend their play value greatly.

Several companies now manufacture large rectangular blocks made of sturdy cardboard. Purchased as flat sheets with detailed folding instructions, they rely on the egg carton principle for their strength: a single block can hold up to two hundred pounds. Because of their light weight and large size, they frequently become trains for children to ride on, sofas and beds for them to lounge on, garages and farms for their larger trucks and animals, or small houses in which to hide.

Aimed at the small child's love of movement, large blocks designed to peg into each other and onto wheel bases offer interesting possibilities. These are expensive, however, and require extensive storage space. Such toys are especially effective in nursery school or day care center settings, where they can be reused every day in different forms.

A popular modification of the kindergarten block idea is a set of wide interlocking tracks. Made of wood, they will not warp, nor will their connectors break off. They are easily assembled, so the budding engineer can make yards of intricate rail or roadways to use in conjunction with blocks and miniatures, creating a city.

3. Boxes

The versatile box is a simple and delightful addition to countless other toys. Small boxes can become medical kits, miniature lions' cages, vehicles. (Crayons or felt-tip markers can aid this transformation; animal cracker boxes with bottle-cap chimneys make wonderful circus trains.) Topless shoe boxes form the rooms of a hotel, beds for dolls, play toasters. Wooden or plastic milk crates or laundry baskets can become lookout points, boats, dungeons.

That wonderfully adaptable major-appliance box makes a fine hideout. Doors and windows can be cut out by parents with scissors or knife. (If you make the windows round and outline squares around them with marking pens, you will retain the strength of the structure.) A coat of shellac helps to preserve the box outdoors. Give small children their own special place to serve as a jail for the outlaw, a post office for a mailman, a cozy spot for a tea party. A large box also serves as a fine play stove, sink or refrigerator. Appropriate markings, and knobs or dials from discarded adult effects, transform them into a source of endless pleasure. For snow days, a box can become the basis of an igloo or a snow fort. Replacement is easy when the box finally wears out.

4. Toy Vehicles

Children love anything that implies motion. Cars, buses, trucks, road graders, dump trucks, steam shovels, trains, motorcycles, airplanes and boats intrigue the young child, who still tends to find magic in movement. Miniatures are useful with blocks and other structures; medium-sized vehicles can carry dolls and animals and cargo and are particularly easy for the small child to manipulate; large ones in which he can ride himself give him play power to rule the world. A sturdy tricycle is indispensable. All vehicles of any size should be sturdy (few things are as useless as a truck missing half its wheels) because they must rely on the child for their go-power. A battery-operated hook-and-ladder truck may fascinate the adult and catch a youngster's eye for a short while, but it deprives the child of an important goal of play: control over his make-believe world. Nothing is more wasteful than expensive "moving" monster toys or complicated trucks cast aside and found useless within a few days of their purchase.

Smaller vehicles vary from scale models of London buses and jet planes to natural wooden fire engines detailed only by a red ladder. As yet there is little research evaluating the relative merits of the more and the less realistic toys in stimulating the imagination of preschool children. Lacking strong evidence, our goal is broad: make a variety of toys available, watch the way they are used, and let the child enjoy the bus that also is used as a camper, the train that carries passengers one day and cotton bales or hay the next, and the plane that serves alternately as a cross-country jet and a fighter-bomber. Large vehicles designed for the child run the gamut in detail and price. A ride-it truck, suitable for zooming around indoors or out, can enliven countless situations; it is alternately a car driving to the library, a rocket to the moon or a motorcycle heading for California.

Stationary vehicles, also boxlike in structure but with room for two to five children, come equipped with one or more steering wheels and their own possibilities. They are expensive for home use, but their equivalent is easily improvised by lining up a few chairs or a piano bench, or laying large blocks end to end. Indoors or out, a barrel or anything else a child can straddle becomes instant transportation with the addition of a toy steering wheel and those precious knobs and dials fastened to a wood or cardboard "control panel."

5. Tables and Chairs

Along with blocks and a tricycle, a child-size table and a suitable seat are basic equipment in a preschool child's world. They can be purchased ready-made or improvised from wire-cable spools of varying sizes, or old doors with screw-in legs. Cardboard cartons can be adapted for short-term use, though something more permanent is desirable unless the replacement supply is limitless. And perhaps most flexibly, they can be modeled after the block concept. Two interesting items on the market using this principle are large polyethylene or wooden cubes open at one end, and the variously named structures that have three sides and a "shelf" or "seat" somewhere in the middle. Some come with slots for easy carrying. Based on a fifteen- or sixteen-inch-square module, they make good tables and chairs, stepstools, cars, boats, trains, beds, and more.

A table surface plus a chair or its equivalent are invaluable for tea parties, playing restaurant or school, as a receptionist's or nurse's desk. On its side, the table can become a stable or a puppet theater. With a sheet or blanket over it, it turns into an instant hideout. And of course, it helps the child be comfortable while doing artwork, devising props, assembling puzzles, building with small pieces or playing board games.

6. Screens

An often intriguing though rather expensive toy structure is the wooden or hardboard (not the cardboard version, please!) three-paneled screen. Several companies make a model that has a "window" opening, chalkboard side panels and a shelf. Used with simple props, it can be alternately a puppet theater, a supermarket, a post office, a bank teller's window, a country cottage. One of the interesting features of the screen is that it is rarely used by a single child; its very structure seems to demand at least two participants. Screens are particularly useful for a school setting. If too expensive to buy, you can make one using plywood panels, 3′ × 3′, or 4′ × 4′, fastened together by four hinges to a panel. Be sure it is stable to prevent its falling over.

7. Make-Believe Creatures

DOLLS AND STUFFED ANIMALS: When nobody is around to play the role of baby or brother, patient or audience, a doll or stuffed animal can fill the bill. It can become a companion or adversary, be tended or attacked, and take on all manner of personalities, depending upon what the child requires at the moment. The wide variety of dolls and animals on the market attests to their eternal popularity among children. Which to choose depends upon the individual child's tastes and preferences. However, the less a doll does by itself, the more conducive it will be to make-believe play. The child who decides what words a doll will utter and in which voice, or where and how the doll will move, is in true control of his play situation. Movable limbs are useful; battery-operated abilities are not. The centuries-old rag doll, and modern factory or homemade variations with floppy limbs and eyes that do not shut, continue to charm their way into the play lives of young children. Sometimes a favorite doll or stuffed animal becomes a child's "security blanket" and is kept for many years. This favorite toy acts as the stimulus for many games, and a source of psychological support.

PUPPETS: Puppets are alternate mouthpieces for a child. Sold at prices from under a dollar to over ten, they can resemble familiar cartoon or television characters, fairy tale personages, people in their everyday roles, animals, monsters. They are made of plastic, paper, plush fabric and rubber. They may be small enough for one finger or large enough for the entire hand. Those that require that the head be moved by one or two inserted fingers are usually too difficult for the young child to handle. More than is the case with many other toys, the child's attitude toward puppets may rest on his parents' willingness to play with them also. Best of all, puppets can easily be made at home from a discarded sock or mitten, sticks or paper, cardboard tubes or sponges.

MINIATURE PEOPLE: Miniature people, suitable as accessories for block structures, dollhouses and oilcloth play environments (with actual rooms painted on the cloth), are not necessarily tiny versions of more standard dolls. Children are fascinated by "people" painted on plastic or wooden double spools, wooden ice cream cup spoons, egg-shaped cylinders, cardboard three-dimensional backgrounds, even small block-like structures. They are available at low cost from several manufacturers and children use them to fill all sorts of roles and personalities. Their portability places them on the "must" list of toys for young children. They make ideal stocking-stuffers for Christmas!

8. Play Places, Costumes and Props

HOUSEHOLD CORNER: Very few accessories for successful doll or house play need actually be bought. Cartons can be fashioned into appliances and doll beds, tables and chairs; a sofa or chair can double as a child's bed or an examining table. A few purchases which do seem to get long mileage in pleasure include tea sets, miniature pots and pans, and a toy telephone. The tea sets and pots and pans serve extra duty in water play, sand play, restaurant games, "picnics." The telephone is used for a game of library or dentist's office. Additional equipment for house and other dramatic play can be scavenged from household drawers, kitchen cabinets, closets. Some suggestions appear at the beginning of this chapter.

HATS AND DRESS-UP CLOTHES: Some children develop hat mania. They are fascinated by the instant identity the donning of a hat provides. With one simple accessory they become firemen, cowboys, construction workers, clowns, Indians, royalty, brides, railroad engineers, baseball or football players, policemen, doctors, nurses, soldiers, sailors, astronauts, majorettes, mailmen, pilots, chefs and more. An old bonnet, hood, beret or fedora can lead a child to assume roles of babies, artists, detectives, or nursery rhyme and fairy tale characters, or the coveted status of mother or father.

Other dress-up paraphernalia ranges from a tinfoil sheriff's badge or dish-towel Batman cape to a converted negligee–ball gown complete with discarded jewelry. Parental ties, belts, scarves and pocketbooks all suggest multiple uses. Old clothes and sheets lend themselves to improvisation, and a discarded white shirt makes a fine uniform for a doctor, dentist, nurse, artist or waitress. Many of these dress-up articles endure for years. A four-year-old may wear a cowboy hat for weeks on end. A once-beloved odd hat may be tucked in a drawer and saved into adult life as a memento of a happy childhood.

MAKEUP: Makeup offers a young child endless delight. Whether it is a mustache or scar drawn with a bit of charcoal or the total exaggeration of a clown, children find the conversion of their faces into those of pirates, cowboys, gypsies, princesses and Indians great fun. A thin layer of cold cream under the artwork helps ease cleansing later on; a mirror in which to view the metamorphosis is essential.

9. Dollhouses and Other Premade Structures

Dollhouses lend themselves to make-believe play. If they have open sides or an open top, the small child can easily manipulate the play people and possessions he chooses to use with them. If the walls are unadorned—at least one model has movable partitions—the child can become an instant decorator by making paintings on index file cards, bottle cap sculptures, rugs cut from fabric pieces or carpet remnants.

Another dollhouse with multipurpose play value is built on the box concept. Wooden rectangles with one open side stack for an apartment house, become wings of an airport, make barns and stables for a farm, turn into houseboats on a cloth sea, complement each other as police station, firehouse and supermarket in a make-believe city. The miniatures the child uses with the structures are, again, determinants of the hour's activities. Shoe boxes are a fine, less permanent substitute. Prices for dollhouses range from moderate to astronomical, but a modestly priced house generally brings great pleasure to a child.

10. Play Environments

There are numerous miniature play environments on the market, including plastic and cardboard airports, farms, zoos, arks, dollhouses, ranches, filling stations and garages. They come complete with play people dressed for the activity and appropriate furniture and accessories. Much more structured than child-designed block or box environments, they can be a stimulant to children just beginning to build their make-believe skills. Care should be taken, however, to select those toys that are very sturdy and, ideally, have provision for storage of their accessories.

A newly organized concept for combining playthings for preschoolers has been developed by Glen Nemnicht and his collaborators at the Far West Laboratory for Educational Research and Development in San Francisco. The Toy Library consists of a set of carefully graded toys that are designed for children aged three to eight. Beginning with simple cans that conceal objects to be shaken to detect their sounds, proceeding to blocks and cards that help children develop complex abstract thinking, the Toy Library provides liveliness along with learning opportunities. The toys are intriguing for adults and instructions are included to help parents "role-play" like children so they will become more sensitive to the youngsters' reactions to these materials.

For larger indoor play areas, a nursery school in New York City has developed a concept that permits parents and children to work together to build play structures such as stands, play horses, movable walls, and color cards, all for two hundred dollars, a price that may limit its purchase to nursery schools and day care centers. The Googolplex will provide parents or teachers with ideas and instructions if you send a request with a stamped, self-addressed envelope to 140 West End Avenue, New York, N.Y. 10023.

11. Oilcloth and Pegboards

A variation on the instant-environment theme is the ever useful length of oilcloth or, especially for the bed-confined child, the pegboard.

Oilcloth, available in a wide range of colors at low cost, can be spread out on the floor as a sea for pirates and their ships, a desert for Indians to traverse, a base of grass or concrete for a maze of roads or apartment buildings. Markings can be drawn or sewn on, if desired.

The accessories for pegboards may be stuck into the board as the child desires, permitting him to design and redesign whatever he is thinking about.

12. Water

Rare is the small child who does not revel in water play. A plugged-up sink, filled dishpan or entire bathtub can prod a child's imagination indefinitely as he or she pretends to wash dishes, concoct soup, sail the seven seas, do the laundry, bathe the dolls. A tub of water set inside an old tire makes an interesting marina or moat; a few drops of dishwashing detergent in a scrub bucket transforms water into a witch's brew; funnels, sieves and basters become the equipment of a scientist. Among the household gadgets which thus lend themselves to water play are straws for blowing bubbles and plastic squeeze bottles for filling and squirting. One unusual toy worth purchasing is a set of foamlike blocks in several basic shapes which float and stick to each other or to the side of a bathtub when wet. Often sold in infants' toy departments, they are inexpensive and provide progressively intricate possibilities for children up to their teen years.

13. Art Supplies

Crayons are a must for all preschoolers. We prefer large ones that have one flat side to prevent them from rolling off the table. We also suggest introducing your child to clay or play dough. These materials are easy to use and can be pounded, rolled, squeezed and formed into the simple objects within a two-year-old's skill or the more complex forms—baskets, animals, dolls, cars—the five-year-old can replicate.

It's easy to make your own play dough and a great deal cheaper than buying it. Measure two cups of flour into a mixing bowl and add one cup of salt. Slowly add water until the mixture is moist. A drop of cooking oil will smooth the dough mixture, and a tablespoon of vinegar will retard spoilage. In order to improve the smell, you may want to add some fine baby powder to the mixture. Wrap this in plastic for storage in your refrigerator. Food coloring may be used. Both you and your child can make dough on a rainy day. The kneading of the mixture is good for his finger muscles and making his own materials improves his sense of pride.

Finger paints are worth the investment because of the pleasure they provide, and the paint can be easily washed off floor, face and clothing. Paper may be large sheets of inexpensive newsprint, shelving paper or special finger paint paper. The three- and four-year-old child may be ready for tempera paints, felt-tip markers or the squeeze paints that come in small tubes with felt stoppers. Your three-year-old will also appreciate a chalkboard and a collection of colored chalk sticks. The four- and five-year-old will enjoy experimenting with other ways of using paint. We suggest using substitutes for paintbrushes, such as feathers, a lamb's-wool roller or a brayer (a special roller to spread ink). Stamp pads and stamps are also fun, especially if you use stamps that come in shapes of animals or figures. Children like to begin thinking about letters and numbers when they are four or five, and printing sets with pads and number and letter stamping blocks seem to help cognitive skills. They are enjoyable supplies when the child role-plays doctor, teacher, salesperson.

Household items such as macaroni, drinking straws (for bracelets and necklaces) and pipe cleaners can be made into dolls, animals and geometric forms. Buttons can be puppets' features, wool scraps dolls' hair. Shiny magazine covers can be cut out and used for collage work. Popcorn can be pasted into animal shapes. The cardboard tubes from toilet paper and paper towels are good for horns and telescopes, telephones and pirate spyglasses. They can be painted easily or covered with scraps of colored paper that are pasted on. Empty plastic containers make good piggy banks when painted or bound around with colored string that can be given a lacquer coating or glue.

14. Lenses

Keep instruments such as a magnifying glass, a microscope if you can afford one, a kaleidoscope, tinted plastic eyeglasses, three-dimensional viewers and binoculars on a shelf. It's exciting for a child to find a small object and see it magnified. Binoculars are fun for the adventure games, such as pirate, camping, cowboys and Indians. Telescopes are expensive, but if you can afford a small one, a child can watch the stars at night.

Outdoor Play Areas: New Environments for Play

Playground architecture has been developing in new and imaginative directions, challenged by the need in city settings and housing developments for equipment that is safe, durable and conducive to imaginative play. Architects have developed ingenious new concepts that break away from the traditional playground toys of Junglegym and swings, and use new materials or modify popular structures such as the sliding pond so that they can yield more fun with less hazard. (See Appendix C.)

New kinds of large-scale outdoor toys include "life-size" Tinker Toy sets so children can create their own outdoor environments. There are many novel climbing houses so designed that some children can clamber on the outside while others are playing quieter games within.

Architects in Sweden, Denmark and Canada have been trying to establish settings that give opportunities not only for mastery of rules games but also for free and make-believe play. These can be applied to the backyard, nursery school recreation areas, housing development and park playgrounds. They include playhouses with slides, old-fashioned hand pumps, hammocks made of old auto tires, hill glides, outdoor storage cupboards, hose-filled play streams and many other devices that a family or a small group of cooperating parents can construct.

We offer the following simple plan for your backyard Fantasy Playground.

1. Landscape

A low fence or natural enclosure of bushes or hedges is ideal for your playground to facilitate supervision of preschoolers and provide for their safety. A site with a small hill and with at least one tree for shade and for a swing certainly will add to the enjoyment of the play area. A sunny area will be welcome if you want to encourage a small garden; be sure you choose an area where you can have a digging spot.

2. Sandboxes

A small sandbox with a hinged cover is practical. This keeps the sand dry and deters nearby pets from entering the box or soiling the sand.

3. Playhouses, Tree Houses, Caves

A playhouse, bought or homemade, is a welcome asset. We don't suggest a fancy house, but it should have three sides and a roof. This becomes the fort, clubhouse, store, cave, pirate's den, castle and witch's house. A small tree house for children of five and six may be built, if it is not too high and if it is sturdily constructed. Children will transform any natural rock formations into all sorts of adventure places.

Young children who are fortunate enough to have a playhouse consider it the king of outdoor equipment. Whether it is an elaborate log cabin or some boards secured to a tree, the playhouse provides a perfect setting for all sorts of dramatic play. Within the freedom of their private preserve, children let their imaginations go. Decorating the playhouse presents the child with a rewarding challenge. Further, it can offer the child a "special place" where he can go when he wishes to be alone. Since we believe that such opportunities are essential to the child's growth and well-being, anything that helps provide them is a welcome situation. There is a special excitement for a child who can crawl or climb into a small enclosed space and be in a world of his own.

4. Swinging

Make sure your swing, whether an old tire hung from a tree or a simple wooden or plastic seat swing, is in an area where other children are not continuously passing by, and that there is adult supervision. A swing for a preschooler should be low—one foot above the ground and hung on five feet of rope. Periodically test the strength of swings that you make from rope to be sure that they will continue to support a child and that the rope is sturdy enough to resist weather's abuse and has not frayed.

5. Animals

A pet rabbit in a cage makes a good addition to the playground. Children like to pet and feed animals, and the care and nurturing of a small creature helps a child understand nature and develop some sense of responsibility. If you do have a rabbit, remember to provide an indoor place for him when the weather gets colder.

6. Loose Equipment

Use your judgment as to the amount of equipment you need, depending upon whether it is meant for a few children or for a nursery school. The play area should be provided with at least one wagon, splinter-free wooden boxes of different sizes and shapes, a two-step ladder, a sawhorse, an old tire, clothesline and clothespins, old pots and pans, and dress-up clothes and hats. Have materials for carpentry such as pieces of wood, hammer, saw, nails, and paintbrushes and latex paint for painting wood, the clubhouse or wooden planks or boxes. Keep these outdoor supplies, which are sold commercially, in a weatherproof metal box or shed.

As mentioned earlier, good equipment for outdoor play includes tricycles, wagons, platform trucks, wheelbarrows, barrels and large hollow building blocks. We would add sawhorses, ladders, planks, tires, and climbing equipment. Toys and materials made of polyethylene do well outside. Inexpensive hoops, plastic play tubes, simple fishing poles, child-sized rakes and shovels and jump-ropes make good accessories.

7. A Place for Adults

You will want a small bench and table in the play area for visiting or supervising adults. If your yard is securely fenced in, you may be able to stay indoors, but always keep a watchful eye, and be sure that you stay in a room that overlooks the play area.

8. Large Indoor-Outdoor Construction Toys

There are many large construction toys that are suitable for both indoor and outdoor use. With the exceptions of the giant Tinker Toys and large hollow wooden blocks, they are usually made from lightweight, waterproof polyethylene. This material has been used successfully in making giant blocks based on both the stacking and the interlocking principles. Two more unusual models, one in twenty-three-inch-square pieces and the other in thirty-inch-square modules, rely for their rigidity on fitting notched sides together. Because of the size of these products, children usually prefer to work together in creating a playhouse, a school or a hospital, often with two or more "rooms." The thirty-inch "snap wall" features circle cutouts in each square, handy as doors, windows, escape hatches.

Construction toys of all sizes have significant value in helping children develop muscle coordination and spatial concepts, and in the larger sizes, offer opportunities for them to learn to cooperate with each other. Their value in stimulating make-believe play is also great, but the child may need adult help from time to time. The child will often begin his construction as a house, road system or camping lodge necessary for his play and then find himself unable to complete his plans. A suggestion of cardboard tubes available for logs in the truck he does not know how to fill, or play people he might need to populate his village, can help him keep his play moving. It is important that the adult respect what the child believes he is constructing and make suggestions appropriate to his ideas. Keep such suggestions to a minimum; the point is to get over the bottleneck.

A related problem occurs when one or more children are building and another child wants to join their play. Children usually have resources of their own for dealing with this situation, but if the adult is aware of the theme of the play and the entering child seems to be having a difficult time, it can be helpful to suggest a role he could assume that would coordinate with the play of the others. Thus, he might be encouraged to fill a wagon or shopping bag with newspapers and "sell" them to the family in the castle, or to use a tricycle as an ice cream truck from which to offer pretend popsicles to the "firemen" worn out from their latest emergency, or to take up a toolbox and don a hard hat and help the group overcome a "plumbing problem." The parent or teacher can be useful to the three- and four-year-olds who are just getting the hang of elaborate make-believe with toys. Beyond five, adults are much more likely to be seen as intruders.

9. Real Vehicles

By far the most treasured outdoor vehicle is the tricycle. It can take a doctor on his rounds, a grownup to work, a nurse to the hospital. One child we know turns her tricycle upside down, using one pedal as a popcorn machine and the other as an ice cream maker. A group of children with tricycles may improvise a gas station or car wash or convoy. A bell or a horn is a useful accessory.

Wagons, platform trucks, shopping carts and four-wheeled wheelbarrows are also fun outside. They can help the newspaper boy make his deliveries, the lumberjack carry his logs, the housewife do her marketing, the hunter carry his prey back to camp. Wagons can carry animals on a "circus train," dolls on a "school bus," people in an "ambulance."

10. Water

Outside, water play becomes freer. A garden hose is helpful for playing car wash, fireman, plumber. A spray nozzle attachment lends itself to elaboration on these themes and others as it becomes a cosmic ray gun, a rainstorm during a camping trip, a fountain. A wading pool is a place for sea divers, sailing to China, splashdown. A bucket of water with a wide paintbrush enables a child to paint fences, houses, cars. A tub resting on two orange crates is the right height for your preschooler. Sailing boats in the tub and washing doll clothes or toys is fun on very hot days. If the child has been encouraged to develop elaborate make-believe plots, there is less likelihood that the water will be used in aimless splashing or as an aggressive material.

11. Sand

Another neutral material beloved by children of all ages is sand. Although special containers are designed for in-house use, a dishpan of salt is probably a preferable substitute for all but the most patient parent. Outdoors, however, sand play offers myriad opportunities. The footprints a child discovers his feet make in sand can become the marks of a dinosaur. His feet and legs can be buried until they disappear, and then emerge as if by magic. Cakes and pies and cookies can be "baked" in plastic and foil containers of all shapes and decorated with sticks for candles, stones for raisins, shells for frosted flowers. Old spoons and forks can help create intricate roadways; buckets or margarine containers can form the basis of elaborate buildings. A two-foot shovel may be useful for excavation at the beach; a few construction trucks for engineering feats at home.

Containers for sand are just as flexible. One of the most delightful is an old rowboat if you can find one and have room for it. The seats not only provide a place for a child to base himself, but serve to keep children's sand constructions separate if they so desire. The boat itself has obvious play possibilities. Barring such a find, sandboxes or pits can be built or bought. The sturdiness of the material and the number of children likely to use it at once should be considerations in your choice.

12. Dirt

Outdoor play must include mention of dirt. Parents fortunate enough to have a large measure of tolerance and a dirt pile in the backyard will find that with child-size shovels on hand, the young members of the family and their friends are likely to turn themselves into a road gang, campers, buried-treasure hunters and farmers. Digging dirt is hard work and the child permitted to master its challenge is likely to feel strong and proud. Again, if the child is helped to develop interesting plot lines and make-believe games, there is less likelihood that the dirt will get thrown at the house or at other children. Children can also be encouraged to plant a small vegetable or flower garden in addition to simply playing in the dirt.

Permanent Outdoor Structures

1. Climbing, Jumping, Sliding

Climbing, swinging, running, jumping, sliding, balancing: these are natural activities of young children. If necessary, they will use trees, cellar ramps, old tires tied to strong branches, curbs, low walls and fences, but playground equipment designed for just such needs can be stimulating. It ranges from inexpensive swing sets to elaborate climbers costing several hundred dollars. Within limits, the better the quality of the materials used and the more children it can hold, the more expensive the item. Considering that a simple swing set or climber is used by children from two years of age to nine or ten, investing in materials that will last out the needs of the family makes some sense.

Among the more conventional items on the market, swings are still a childhood favorite. Children can mount them and go to Mars, pretend they are rides at an amusement park, use them as height for a "parachute jump," make believe they are flying, or be acrobats on their crossbars. A glider or lawn swing makes a handy train; a monkey swing conjures up visions of safaris.

A pole for sliding and climbing may be embedded in cement in the ground. At least eighteen inches of a four- or five-foot pole should be underground. A stepstool near the pole helps the child get to the top for his slide down. Although slides are often appended to swing sets for home use, they tend to be isolating; it is nearly impossible for several children to enjoy them at once. At least one manufacturer has risen to the occasion and now sells a slide that is free-standing and therefore usable indoors as well as out; it has a 4' × 8' surface, allowing four or more children to use it at once. Outdoor architects are increasingly exploring very wide steps and slides so that several children can go up and down without fighting for space.

Another type of slide that deserves mention is the small wooden construction with the steps up one side, the ramp on the other, and an enclosure in the middle. When preschoolers no longer find its height a challenge, they are likely to prop the ramp up on a chair and thus create a playhouse, throw blankets over it for caves, use the hideout as a refuge in games of cops and robbers. Children up to the ages of eight and nine have been known to devise new uses for the structure.

A modern variation of the seesaw or rocker is made in polyethylene, thus suitable for inside use or out; and because it is lightweight, it is easily flipped over so that a tunnel is formed. Made in widths designed to hold either one child or two on either end, it suggests boats, buses or stagecoaches. The larger model becomes stairs on one side, slide on the other when it is turned over; the smaller one reveals two sliding surfaces.

Climbers vary from a rope ladder attached to a tree to huge creations meant for elementary school playgrounds. If the buyer bears in mind durability and the superior play value of a toy that can be used cooperatively by several children at once, his fancy and pocketbook are good guides to selection. The openings in the middle of even the simple structures can be makeshift clubhouse, prison or zoo. Ropes for trapezes, bridges (all rope or with wooden slats), pulley rides, and ropes that hang free from a tree or are stretched horizontally for climbing, encourage all sorts of adventure play as well as skills in coordination.

Large standing traffic signs are fun. And, again, the box is perhaps most versatile of all. Wooden boxes open at one end and large enough for a child to crawl into can be houses or tents, mountains or stages. With a narrow board spanning them, they transform a three-year-old into a tightrope walker; with a wide board, they form tunnels and shopping malls.

Using Television Constructively
for Imaginative Growth

In most homes in America, television is virtually a member of the family. The average young child in the United States grows up reacting not only to the words and facial expressions and movements of his parents and brothers and sisters, but also to those of the odd little people who move across the screen in the living room, bedroom, kitchen or family room.

This is new to the life of growing children and to our culture. In the past, the major influences on young children were the immediate caretakers who fed and watched over them. They learned about the "outside world" from the stories they heard from their mothers or grandmothers, or the accounts of the day's work somewhere out in the world they overheard from fathers, grandfathers or older brothers and sisters. Today this world is brought to them, together with a surprising amount of information and emotional material, by the box that sits in everyone's home. On one channel the child sees a group of high-kicking chorus girls in an old Busby Berkeley musical, on another a baseball game in which men throw balls and hit them with a stick, and on a third scenes of people in a strange junglelike land beating drums, jumping up and down with spears and shields, and wearing very little clothing.

What is your child to make of all this? How do diverse scenes and people and information become a part of the day-to-day imagination of the child? Is there an approach to using the television set effectively to help a child grow up with a constructive and creative imaginative capacity?

There are a few parents who determined right from the outset that they would not expose their children to television and simply banned it from their homes. In some instances we know of, this policy worked out extremely well. The children reared without TV developed flexible imaginative capacities and scarcely seemed to miss the set at all. But most people are not prepared to go this far. Parents like to watch television themselves and find it a great relief from the day's pressures. Many women who stay home as homemakers are quite used to having the set turned on as they go about their chores. If there are toddlers around when the TV is working, they will obviously get used to looking at it.

It is our personal belief that it would be better for children's development if they saw no TV at all until they were of school age, with well-established habits of reading. Parents or teachers at preschool would have no difficulty in providing them with many imaginative resources without TV. But enforcing a complete ban on television is very difficult today. We recognize that 99 percent of the parents will have no such inclination. Therefore, it makes sense to accept television and try to find out how to make the best use of this extremely powerful medium.

What Psychologists Have Learned About Television and Its Effect on Children

More than 90 percent of the homes in America have television sets and these sets are usually turned on more than three hours a day. It is only in the last ten years or so that behavioral scientists have had the opportunity to do any reasonably careful research on how television affects growing children. It is useful to review briefly some of the major findings.

Television Violence and Children

Many parents or citizens' groups such as Action for Children's Television (ACT) have called attention to the possibility that children will be encouraged to become too aggressive as a result of the amount of violent activity they witness on television. Careful monitoring of the frequency of violence shown on television indicates that this fear is justified. There are often as many as three acts of violence every few minutes on view at times when children are likely to watch. Many parents do not pay enough attention to what their children are viewing and even allow them to see later evening programs, in which violence is so prevalent.

Considering the vast number of incidents on television of fighting, shooting and other aggressive acts, it is obvious that only a small percentage is imitated by children or we would be living in a state of perpetual warfare! Nevertheless, a number of very careful research studies have demonstrated quite conclusively that young children, *especially those who have already been active in hitting other children,* will increase their aggressive behavior after viewing even simple-minded cartoons such as *Batman.* An extremely important study carried out over a period of ten years in upstate New York demonstrated that the amount of violence exhibited by young adults by the time they were eighteen to twenty could be best explained (among all other factors studied) by the amount of television violence they had viewed as children. Every parent and nursery school teacher can give examples of children coming to school after having watched particular television shows, and running amok in acts of physical aggression directed toward other children. During the 1970s nursery school and kindergarten teachers have complained very frequently about the effects of movies and television programs such as *Kung Fu.* Whatever the producer's intentions, whether entertainment or moralizing, most relatively young children retain from such programs the odd movements, the grunts and shouts, and the vigorous kicks that characterize the hero's ability to beat up the "bad guys" in the end. Kung Fu kicks or karate chops, faked painlessly on TV, can hurt when delivered by five-year-olds to unsuspecting children in the adjoining block corner.

In these numerous experiments over the past ten years, the results point up again and again the fact that children do imitate aggressive acts. Even gentle Mister Rogers, of public television's *Mister Rogers' Neighborhood,* had to modify a small gimmick he used at the beginning of his show. He would throw his sneaker up into the air and catch it. Too many children, imitating this, got hit on the head.

Frightening Scenes and Night Terrors

We all know that monster movies and the supernatural have great appeal for youngsters. But many parents are not sensitive to the fact that what is exciting and enjoyable to a child at one age may be terrifying and cause nightmares for a younger child. Teen-agers are attracted to monster shows because though they are initially frightened by some of the suspense and danger of the film, they have sufficient experience in life to know that this is merely a movie and that such monsters do not exist. They can be brought to the brink of fear and then back off from it, feeling grown up about their wisdom and reacting with laughter.

But children between two and five do not have anything remotely like the background of information or the thinking capacity to deal with such strange events. While they may be initially fascinated by the strangeness of a monster's appearance, their subsequent reaction will be one of terror and there are many instances in which nightmares, night terrors and fear of the dark have been caused by such viewing. Parents must learn to be very sensitive to what their children can tolerate and at what age levels such scenes are manageable. To this day many adults who grew up in the age of movies but before television can recall the frightening effects of particular scenes even in relatively harmless films such as *Snow White and the Seven Dwarfs* or the much-loved *The Wizard of Oz.*

On television the child is exposed to dozens and dozens of frightening scenes and monster movies. Because it is hard to predict in advance which particular ones will have a special effect on your children, parental judgment is very important. A number of years ago there was a soap opera called *Dark Shadows,* built around supernatural themes with zombies and vampires, which appeared regularly on national television in midafternoon. Many children below school age who watched it with older brothers or sisters were extremely frightened by it.

One of the problems of young children is that when they go to sleep at night, they have no intellectual or cognitive structures to reassure them about the darkness and the strange play of shadows and lights across the room. The temptation is to attribute such phenomena to mysterious or supernatural forces, bogey men, goblins or monsters. Add to these the many, many sinister characters from television or movies to which they may have been exposed, and one can see how easily the imagination of the child can be led into frightening paths. Programs that have deliberately developed suspense and terror as part of their format are very disturbing to them.

Constructive Possibilities of Television

So far we have been stressing some of the risks inherent in the television-viewing situation for younger children. But television has many other possibilities as well. As the psychologist Robert Liebert has said, it does open "a window on the world."

For children who lack the advantages of being told stories or of having parents who read to them regularly, it introduces much useful information about geography, cultural mythology and history.

Television plays a very important part in stimulating the imagination as well. Many of the make-believe games that children play in nursery school use characters and themes, scenes and plots that have been at least in part suggested by what they have watched on television. Children learn all kinds of things from the television medium, from the commercial jingles that have by now become a part of our culture and folklore to the fascinating characters who represent so many different eras of history or parts of the world. And depending on the nature of the programming, children can also absorb many important social values from television.

An increasing number of careful researches have shown that children do acquire reading readiness and number skills from watching programs like *Sesame Street.* They have also been shown to become more helpful, friendly and cooperative after watching programs like *Mister Rogers' Neighborhood.* In our own research we have observed that three- and four-year-old children increased their imaginative skills and the sheer joy of play after watching such a program, particularly if an adult was sitting with them while they watched. Television *can* be stimulating and helpful for the child's development in many important ways, provided that the programming is geared to the children's level of understanding and also provided that parents control what children watch.

Helping Your Child to Watch Intelligently

Sometime between the ages of one and one and a half, your child will become increasingly aware of the existence of the television set, and will show some reactions to it. A child at this age may not pause in front of the set very long and certainly will have difficulty in comprehending what is going on. Still, it may not be too early for you to give consideration to initiating the child into a TV orientation that will keep viewing under control and minimize its dangers. This may mean thinking through for yourself the whole household's viewing patterns. The same is true in the case of the use of television sets in day care centers and nurseries. All too often the availability of a set leads to its being left on for an excessive period; it becomes an easy way to keep children occupied. The same concern needs to be exercised in the case of baby-sitters or older brothers or sisters who are watching younger children.

It is important in a household with young children not to keep television on unless somebody is actively watching. If you have older children it is also important to make sure that you know what they are watching while a much younger child is around. This will be particularly difficult for you to manage if you do not start your children early with some fairly firm rules about what times and under what circumstances they can watch television. Many parents take the easy way out and avoid initial conflicts by simply holding the child on their lap while they watch their own favorite programs, whether daytime game shows, soap operas or evening situation comedies or detective shows. What we are recommending is that as the child is eased into television viewing, the viewing rules and the kinds of shows permissible be made very clear right from the start.

Sometime when the child is one and a half to two, it will be very useful for one of the parents to get into a regular habit of watching a specific show with the child. Choose a program that is very carefully geared toward children, with a set time, so that a very definite pattern of day-to-day viewing can be established. By the age of two to two and a half, a child ought to know that there is a special show and a special time for television which will be shared with mother or father, grandma or grandpa, or a baby-sitter. That show should be one directed toward very young children of preschool age, such as *Sesame Street, Captain Kangaroo* and *Mister Rogers.* These programs tailor their vocabulary to the very young, they include humor and novelty, they have recurring central characters who are likable, and they avoid violence or frightening scenes.

You should screen shows in advance, to decide which you will use for regular viewing with your child. Watch it a few times by yourself, and try to get a feeling for it. Begin with a show like *Captain Kangaroo* or *Mister Rogers' Neighborhood.* These programs have sufficient variety and interest for the very young child and lack the rapid-fire, almost helter-skelter quality of *Sesame Street.* Do not expect to be greatly entertained by them yourself, though after a while they can grow on you, particularly if you see that your child is enjoying them. The humor and the sugary quality of the characters may put you off, particularly if you have a fairly worldly view of life, but give your child a chance to start out on a simpler and sweeter level!

These comments are not meant to be facetious. Most child specialists agree that it is especially important for a toddler to experience consistency, a certain regularity of presentation, to be freed from the negative implications of situations, and to perceive only the most positive and constructive aspects of day-to-day living. This helps establish a beginning identity for the child, a *basic trust* (as that great student of the life cycle Erik Erikson put it) which will enable him or her to move freely to explore newer and newer experiences. The child who begins in a world in which hopes are constantly frustrated, in which the fearful aspects of human relationships are called to attention, will become afraid to try new experiences and explore the world, and will develop a stunted and dour view of self and others.

Once you have decided on a program, you can invite your child in to sit with you on your lap or near you, keeping in mind

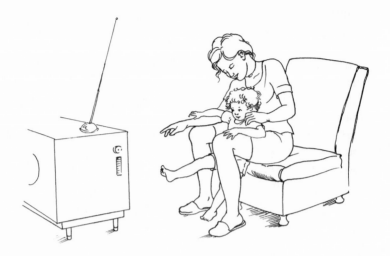

that children are wriggly and have short attention spans. Certainly between ages one and a half and two and a half the child may not pay more than intermittent attention to the show. The parents' job here is certainly not to force viewing. Rather, the parent should simply turn the show on and sit quietly with the child. If the child begins to roam around the room don't intervene. Occasionally a remark such as "Look what's happening over there" might be useful to the child to help him grasp a point that is being made. This is also valuable in helping the child identify with the adult who is viewing regularly with him, and share some positive experiences and interests.

Do not expect even a three- or four-year-old to stay put throughout a half-hour or hour-long television show. Your role must be one of encouraging the child to notice the interesting aspects of the program without trying to force him or her to pay attention. If you pressure the child to watch, the experience will of course become a negative one. But children are delighted to have adults who say, "Oh, look at that duck Captain Kangaroo is holding. It's a real duck. What does it sound like?" Here you can attempt to get the child to interact with the object on the screen, and you can explain in simple terms what Captain Kangaroo is doing with the duck. For children in the three- and four-year age span, we have found from our recent research that even Mister Rogers, who very carefully explains every detail of what he is doing and talks directly to the child with great sincerity, may not be fully understood. Having an adult around to help plays an important part in making children more effective viewers.

What to Look For in a Beginning Show

Let us look more closely at the elements a parent or teacher ought to consider in deciding on the kind of viewing advisable for children. These should involve a program in which there is a unifying adult figure, male or female, who conveys a sense of interest in the viewing child, a sense of personal concern and stability. This central figure should not be portrayed as ludicrous or fundamentally ineffective. The pace of the program should be slow enough so that children can savor it. The show must provide sufficient entertainment value in the sense that it has story material, and some opportunities to laugh or to demonstrate unusual sights or objects. The program should also be one that encourages imaginative play on the part of the child apart from the viewing situation. That is, it should have characters the child may want to imitate, and it should also make the distinction between reality and fantasy quite clear to the child. It should avoid grossly frightening or dangerous scenes, or indications of punishment to children or animals. This does not mean that there can be no adventure in the stories. There is ample room for adventure without punishment or serious danger.

While children are greatly entertained by a variety of fantasy characters and make-believe elements, we believe it is important that the first viewing experience be one in which there is a mixture of reality and fantasy in the clearly separated form we have cited. We do not encourage beginning the child's television experience with cartoons, because these are likely to be confusing. Cartoon or fantasy-type material should be presented only *after* a relationship has been firmly established between the child and the live adult on the set who can be identified with as a parent figure of some kind. The TV adult can make the transition to the fantasy world very clear to the child in much the same way that a parent or grandparent says, "Now I am going to tell you a story." This approach helps the child make the transition from the parent who begins by viewing along with the child to the father or mother figure who is the central character of the show. It also allows him to understand gradually that his real parents are tall and live right here, and that the little man in the box is not really inside the television set, but simply represents a picture of another adult *like* mommy or daddy.

Viewing Together

After a while the child may begin to look forward very much to the regular watching time with mommy or daddy. For several months or even longer, it seems to us, a mother or father ought to take the time to sit quietly with the child, watching a particular show. Gradually the child will require less and less of your presence, and you can begin to phase yourself out.

One of the things to watch for is vocabulary. You can help the child in the beginning by defining some of the words used, or demonstrating the terms through movements or gestures. You will be able to phase this out gradually too, because as the child's vocabulary expands he also increases his ability to understand new words through the context in which they emerge. The same attention needs to be paid to emotional and social situations that occur in the little story usually worked into the show.

Here again, to help the child begin to develop some make-believe capacity, you can encourage him to play out some of the stories with you, or help him imitate some of the sound effects or characters' voices.

A father of our acquaintance used to watch *Mister Rogers' Neighborhood* regularly with his three-and-a-half- and two-and-a-half-year-old sons. At points in the story where the character of King Friday the Thirteenth appeared and carried out some rather high-handed actions, the father encouraged the children to see what a funny, pompous fellow the king was. He also brought about a good deal of laughter himself by trying to imitate the king's voice and then encouraged his children to try the same imitation. One time he helped them cut out a gold crown like the one King Friday wore. Each child tried it on and pretended to walk around like the king. After six months of regular viewing the children had learned how to deal with the program effectively, and the father tapered off his viewing. Once in a while the mother came in to see what they were watching and to make some pleasant comments.

The adventures of the characters on the program were discussed at mealtimes by the whole family as pleasant events, but always in the context of the fact that these were television events. This routine of family discussion, like the recounting of dreams, became part of a regular warm interchange that characterized mealtimes.

The procedure we're suggesting has the advantage of making television a positive experience for the child, yet one with very clear boundaries. Children look forward to these viewing times, of course. Some critics may say that we are proposing to "hook" the children on television by this method. Our answer is that the children will be hooked no matter what you do, short of removing the TV set from the home. If this is the case, why not start them off in a psychologically positive way? The whole viewing situation will have begun under circumstances in which the children feel a rapport between themselves and their parents, a rapport which, like dreams and stories, can become the basis for close, shared experiences.

Expanding but Limiting Children's Viewing

Once the child is past the age of two and a half or three, the likelihood is that he will want to view a much greater variety of shows. Again, the adult must first explore the territory and then allow the child to ease into it. Naturally, such viewing cannot be entirely controlled in every home, particularly when there are older brothers and sisters around. But it remains very worthwhile for parents who are interested in leading the child into the healthiest kind of television viewing to preview certain programs and then sit with the child for at least a few of the chosen shows and interact. If the child knows from the start that there are firmly limited times in which television viewing is permitted, and that these times are accompanied by pleasurable reactions from his parents, he will accept the limitation of time as a natural part of his daily life. At other times children can turn to make-believe and fantasy games of the kind encouraged in this volume.

Probably a major expansion of the young child's viewing can be the Saturday-morning children's programs, which now show *relatively* better-thought-out cartoons, at least on the major networks. The networks have been attempting to adapt programming to findings based on psychological investigation of the importance of positive social experience and altruistic or socially helpful behaviors. They have also been trying to reduce violence, at least on Saturday mornings.

The kinds of programs one must be especially on guard against for children between two and five include the following:

1. Programs that involve great danger or threat to animals, to children relatively close in age to the viewing children, or to parent figures. Such programs can generate nightmares and very frightening fantasies.

2. Programs that involve excessive "spookiness" and unexplained supernatural characters, such as monsters engaged in frightening activities.

3. Programs in which there is a considerable amount of direct violence or physical attack. This is especially serious if the children have not yet developed much tendency toward make-believe play, into which they can divert some of their imitative tendencies. Indications are that when violent scenes or incidents of fighting are cast in very remote settings, such as battles between knights or the highly stylized fighting seen in historical movies, there is less likelihood that the children will imitate aggression directly. On the other hand, excessive fighting with fists between young adolescents, battles between children, and scenes of violence within family settings are all likely to produce both terror and imitation.

4. Young children are especially frightened and dismayed by dismemberment. Cartoons in which characters are literally torn apart terrify them. Similarly, scenes in shows involving live adults or children in which there is evidence of physical wounds, mutilation or violent physical contact will be frightening to preschoolers.

5. Athletic or physical activities which are conducive to imitation but extremely risky should be avoided at all costs. The jump by motorcyclist Evel Knievel across a canyon, coming as it did with tremendous publicity, led to a rash of dangerous imitations by young children all around the country. A U.S. Congressman from New York catalogued some fifty cases of accidents to children following this presentation. Any viewing situation of this type must be dealt with by simply playing the material down for the child. If it is viewed by the family, a parent must make it very clear to the child that this is essentially a performance. It is something that a child can imitate only in make-believe ways, with miniature toy cars or objects, but never with his own tricycle.

6. There are occasionally situations in which the whole family

will view programs of a more adult nature. Here again, the material may be distressing to younger children, and it is especially important that the parents play an ameliorating role when they see incidents that are likely to be frightening or to provoke later confusion and night terrors. Even programs that have the best of intentions may unwittingly create dreadful effects on children. A broadcast of CBS's *60 Minutes* dealt with the subject of euthanasia ("mercy killing") for children born grossly deformed or afflicted with gross brain damage. Unknown to her parents, a child of four saw this program. In the next few days at nursery school she was extremely nervous and tearful and asked many questions about death and what happens to children. It emerged that on the TV show she had seen parents wheeling around a child who was described as "practically like a vegetable." The parents themselves said they wished the child would die. From the standpoint of the four-year-old, this baby looked perfectly normal. She could not grasp the discussion about its brain injuries. All she saw, instead, were parents who said that they wished their child would die. Would that be her fate? Did her parents ever talk about things like that? If she broke a leg and had to "walk funny" (as some children on the program were doing), would her parents also say they wished she had died when she was born?

Examples like this indicate some of the genuine perils of television that often go undetected. In this case the parents had no inkling of the fact that their child had been watching, or of the content of the program. Fortunately, alerted by the nursery school, they were able to discuss the situation and clarify it for their child.

What are some of the positive things to look for in programs for the preschooler? We mentioned a few in describing shows like *Mister Rogers' Neighborhood* and *Captain Kangaroo*. Generally we find children will stick with programs like these, if they were enjoyed early, through the ages of four and five. But it will be helpful for them to expand into new shows with varied content and more exposure to the broad range of culture and legend:

1. Programs that tell well-known stories clearly and without adult "show-biz" cynicism are desirable. Fairy tales of the less frightening kind, ancient myths and adventures from history are all much appreciated by four- and five-year-olds.

2. Realistic animal stories can be sources of great delight. Children begin to develop important feelings of love and warmth, as well as a sense of caretaking, when watching accounts of how animals are raised with love by other children. There is ample opportunity for *minor* misadventures and mishaps, which add just enough tension to make for interest without frightening the children.

3. Fairly realistic cartoons that involve stories of small groups of children who band together (whether in a family or as friends) to deal with adventurous circumstances, to build or construct things, or to help other, more unfortunate children, adults or animals can be very effective. These not only entertain but can lead the children into more constructive make-believe play situations.

4. Programs that introduce children to new art forms—music, dance, puppetry—if done with style and pitched so as to be clear, can be extremely stimulating. In our research we observed that a program in which a marionette troupe demonstrated the working of the marionettes and then told the story of Jack and the Beanstalk with them was intensely absorbing and evoked a good deal of subsequent imaginative play by children who watched it in a day care center.

5. Family situation comedies, if viewed with family members, are a possibility. Here it is important that the adults point out similarities and differences relative to one's own family. One must be careful lest the children are exposed to false values, excessive ridiculing of the father as a bumbler or the mother as

a shrew, or to overemphasis on well-to-do surroundings or unusually talented children.

Television Commercials and Your Child

Perhaps more than children in any other part of the world, American children of the past generation have grown up in a world of television commercials that entice, suggest and often demand their interest in and desire for advertised products. Indeed, given the great emphasis placed on premiums, particularly in advertising for cereals, one might say that the child viewing television is subject to bribery dozens of times a day. There are many groups and professionals who feel that any commercial advertising for very young children is potentially harmful. It puts the child in the position of wanting things he cannot evaluate because of his immaturity. The likelihood, however, is that in the immediate future television commercials will continue to be viewed by large numbers of children.

Concern about the control of advertising, taking into account children's limited capacity for understanding, has come from groups within the industry itself, such as the code for producers prepared by the National Association of Broadcasters (NAB), and more recently by a new set of guidelines promulgated by the Children's Advertising Review Unit of the Council of Better Business Bureaus. These guidelines are designed to advise the creative staffs of agencies preparing commercials on what kinds of commercial appeal are grossly unfair or confusing to children, and what types of content may be dangerous. For example, showing children carrying out acts that are really quite risky on moving toys such as tricycles or wagons would be forbidden by such a code. Similarly, in the realm of imagination, a widespread practice in the earlier days of television was to show toys in close-up form, so that they looked extremely large and gave the impression that one could do many things with them which actually were impossible. Children were tremendously attracted to these apparently life-size toys, and deeply disappointed, after a purchase, when they found they were often no larger than one's hand. Often their assemblage required elaborate construction techniques or they were being sold without batteries and couldn't be operated after assembly.

Many of these grosser deceptions are no longer a part of children's advertising, at least on a national scale. Nevertheless, exposure to enticing ads creates problems in itself. The child wants a new cereal because of the premium promised, and then may refuse to eat it or find its taste unpleasant. Parents questioned in various surveys have complained about arguments with their children in the supermarket over the purchase of premium-featuring cereals, which the parents' better judgment suggests the children will not eat. Very often, too, the premiums turn out to be much less appealing than they looked in the lively twenty or thirty seconds they were shown on screen.

Professional groups have recently tried to counsel advertisers to include more emphasis on cooperative behavior, friendliness and good nutrition in commercials. For example, in presentations to groups of advertisers, we have advocated that toys that lend themselves to imaginative and make-believe games be presented by children who are actually playing such games, so as to enhance the likelihood that children will develop interest and skill in make-believe. Parents can also play a role in this, by calling children's attention to toys or objects shown on TV that really will have lasting make-believe value. They can encourage interest in toys that are not set up to serve a single function. A G.I. Joe doll in full regalia can only be a soldier. A boy doll without so explicit a function can be used in many different kinds of imaginative games. Similarly, the most consistently and widely used toys are the blocks, shapes and forms that lend themselves to the construction of a variety of settings around which make-believe play can take place.

Parents and teachers in nursery schools and kindergartens

should take a more active part in encouraging the child to understand that commercials may not always be accurate and are at times even misleading. That means a certain amount of watching of children's television and monitoring of commercials, so that the adult can talk with some authority to the child about these issues.

An example of the kind of advertising that can create problems for a child is a commercial for a group of toys built around a popular television program that involved considerable adventure and had a clearly delineated set of good guys and bad guys. The commercial itself presented a mountainous physical setting as if it were real. The toy figures appeared much larger than they were in reality and as if they could move under their own power. To the watching children, therefore, it seemed as if one could create a great adventure with battles and narrow escapes simply by letting the toy figures jump around on their own. This is, of course, very deceiving to children's expectations. It seems to us that it would have been far more useful and fairer to the child to have shown children manipulating the figures, however crudely, calling out the sound effects that might go with the scene and actually imitating the voices. This would have indicated to children how actively they could use the toys, and also encouraged them in an approach to interesting imaginative play.

The parents' or teachers' role in relation to commercials has to be handled very carefully. Simply to pooh-pooh whatever appears on commercials creates confusion for children. They are too young to be exposed to a cynicism that they can scarcely comprehend, and which may instead create a feeling in them that their parents are negatively oriented. In general the basic principle should be to point out constructively to the child the real advantages and disadvantages of the particular toy. Thus, if there is a toy around the house or nursery school that resembles the advertised item, the parent or teacher should pick up the available toy, show the child how to play with it, and point out its similarities to and differences from the one on the commercial. Here there is an interchange around play that the child will enjoy in itself, and at the same time less chance for the development of the feeling that "grownups are mean about things we see on television."

Many of the toys and other attractive objects shown on television turn out to be more expensive than one has been led to believe. This is especially true when one must get batteries or purchase a whole group of toys, as in the case of sets which involve a fort, Indians, cowboys, background scenery, covered wagons and horses, all of which turn out to be sold separately. One of the things an alert parent might do would be to try to determine to what extent toys of these kinds are already available in the house, or could be improvised or purchased more cheaply. Here again, one can approach the child with a positive attitude, saying, "We're going to try to help you enjoy toys like these, but not the special toys you saw on TV."

Television, Movies and Imagination

Ultimately we must face the fact that we all live today in a world of highly packaged fantasy, a visual panorama of vicarious experiences. The concerned parent or teacher can use the widespread availability of interesting characters and adventures by helping the child to incorporate this material into play and into self-entertainment. The child will welcome adult suggestions about how TV shows or movies seen with the parents can become the basis for make-believe games. Don't be afraid to get down on the floor with a four-year-old and start off a game based on a recently viewed Walt Disney episode or a movie from which you've just returned. The children will soon take over and move the game in their own direction, as we've suggested, and you can phase yourself out. The media then become sources for a whole variety of plots, characters and self-entertainment possibilities. They can feed the imagination rather than substitute for it. If parents and teachers are willing to become partners in play with the children in their care, we may see the flourishing of a new period of imagination and creativity in young and old alike.

Recommended Reading and Listening for Children

BOOKS

Animals

Barrett, Judi. *Animals Should Definitely Not Wear Clothing.* Atheneum, 1971.

Bettinger, Craig. *Follow Me, Everybody.* Doubleday, 1968.

Brooke, Leslie. *Johnny Crow's New Garden.* Warne, 1935.

Burningham, John. *Mr. Gumpy's Outing.* Holt, Rinehart & Winston, 1970.

Carroll, Ruth. *Where's the Bunny?* Walck, 1950.

D'Aulaire, Ingri and Edgar. *Animals Everywhere.* Doubleday, 1954.

De Regniers, Beatrice Schenk. *Cats Cats Cats Cats Cats.* Pantheon, 1958.

_____. *May I Bring a Friend?* Atheneum, 1964.

Ets, Marie Hall. *Elephant in the Well.* Viking, 1972.

_____. *In the Forest.* Viking, 1944.

_____. *Just Me.* Viking, 1965.

_____. *Play with Me.* Viking, 1955.

Fatio, Louise, and Duvoisin, Roger. *The Happy Lion.* McGraw-Hill, 1954.

Flack, Marjorie. *Angus and the Cat.* Doubleday, 1931.

_____. *Ask Mr. Bear.* Macmillan, 1932.

_____. *The Restless Robin.* Houghton Mifflin, 1965.

Friskey, Margaret. *Chicken Little, Count-To-Ten*. Childrens Press, 1946.

Green, Mary McBurney. *Everybody Eats*. Young Scott, 1950.

———. *Everybody Has a House*. Young Scott, 1961.

Hogrogian, Nonny. *One Fine Day*. Macmillan, 1971.

Keats, Ezra Jack. *Over in the Meadow*. Four Winds, 1971.

Rabinowitz, Sandy. *The Red Horse and the Bluebird*. Harper & Row, 1975.

Spier, Peter. *To Market! To Market!* (poems). Mother Goose Library. Doubleday, 1973.

Tworkov, Jack. *The Camel Who Took a Walk*. E. P. Dutton, 1951.

Animals in People Situations

Bennett, Rainey. *The Secret Hiding Place*. World, 1960.

Bond, Michael, and Banberry, Fred. *Paddington Bear*. Random House, 1973.

Brenner, Barbara. *Mr. Tall and Mr. Small*. Young Scott, 1966.

Brunhoff, Jean de. *The Story of Babar* (and sequels). Random House, 1933.

Conford, Ellen. *Impossible Possum*. Little, Brown, 1971.

D'Aulaire, Ingri and Edgar. *Foxie, the Singing Dog*. Doubleday, 1969.

Duvoisin, Roger. *What Is Right for Tulip*. Knopf, 1969.

Minarik, Else Holmelund. *Little Bear* (and sequels). Harper & Row, 1957.

Potter, Beatrix. *The Tale of Peter Rabbit*. Warne, 1903.

Slobodkina, Esphyr. *Caps for Sale*. William R. Scott, 1947.

Waber, Bernard. *Lyle, Lyle, Crocodile*. Houghton Mifflin, 1965.

Birthdays and Holidays

Charlip, Remy. *Fortunately*. Parents' Magazine Pre: ;, 1964.

Keats, Ezra Jack. *A Letter to Amy*. Harper & Row, 1968.

Kraus, Robert. *How Spider Saved Christmas*. Simon & Schuster, 1970.

———. *The Tree That Stayed up Until Next Christmas*. Windmill Books, 1972.

Varga, Judy. *Once-a-Year-Witch*. Morrow, 1973.

Waber, Bernard. *Lyle and the Birthday Party*. Houghton Mifflin, 1972.

Change and Growth

Burton, Virginia Lee. *The Little House*. Houghton Mifflin, 1942.

———. *Mike Mulligan and His Steam Shovel*. Houghton Mifflin, 1939.

Charles, Nicholas. *Jane Anne June Spoon and Her Very Adventurous Search for the Moon*. Norton, 1966.

Gwynne, Fred. *The King Who Rained*. Windmill Books, 1970.

Keats, Ezra Jack. *Jennie's Hat*. Harper & Row, 1966.

Peet, Bill. *The Wump World*. Houghton Mifflin, 1970.

Silverstein, Shel. *The Giving Tree*. Harper & Row, 1964.

Swift, Hildegarde. *The Little Lighthouse and the Big Gray Bridge*. Harcourt, Brace, 1962.

Tripp, Paul. *The Little Red Flower*. Doubleday, 1968.

Creations, Ingenuity, Fantasy

Alexander, Martha. *Blackboard Bear*. Dial Press, 1969.

———. *Maybe a Monster*. Dial Press, 1968.

———. *We Never Get to Do Anything*. Dial Press, 1970.

Anno, Mitsumasa. *Magical Midnight Circus*. Weatherhill, 1972.

———. *Upside-Downers*. Weatherhill, 1971.

Borack, Barbara. *Gooney*. Harper & Row, 1968.

Cameron, Polly. *The Secret Toy Machine*. Coward, McCann & Geoghegan, 1972.

De Regniers, Beatrice Schenk. *William O'Dwyer Jumped in the Fire*. Atheneum, 1968.

Devlin, Wende and Harry. *Aunt Agatha, There's a Lion Under the Couch!* Van Nostrand, 1968.

Frances, Frank. *The Magic Wallpaper*. Abelard-Schuman, 1970.

Gauch, Patricia Lee. *Christina Katerina and the Box*. Coward, McCann & Geoghegan, 1971.

Hitte, Kathryn. *What Can You Do Without a Place to Play*. Parents' Magazine Press, 1971.

Interaction Books, *Things to Make; Whee! I Can Be; Game Songs*. Houghton Mifflin, 1975.

Keats, Ezra Jack. *Hi, Cat!* Macmillan, 1970.

———. *Psst! Doggie*. Watts, 1973.

Keith, Eros. *Nancy's Backyard*. Harper & Row, 1973.

Kraus, Robert. *Milton the Early Riser*. Windmill Books, 1972.

Lear, Edward. *The Quangle Wangle's Hat.* Watts, 1970.

Moffett, Martha. *A Flower Pot Is Not a Hat.* E. P. Dutton, 1972.

Nash, Ogden. *The Animal Garden.* M. Evans, 1965.

Parish, Peggy. *Amelia Bedelia.* Harper & Row, 1963.

Preston, Edna. *Pop Corn and Ma Goodness.* Viking, 1969.

Raskin, Ellen. *Franklin Stein.* Atheneum, 1972.

Reiss, John J. *Colors.* Bradbury, 1969.

Sendak, Maurice. *In the Night Kitchen.* Harper & Row, 1970.

———. *Where the Wild Things Are.* Harper & Row, 1963.

Sherman, Ivan. *Robert and the Magic String.* Harcourt Brace Jovano-
vich, 1973.

Shulevitz, Uri. *One Monday Morning.* Scribner, 1967.

Silverstein, Shel. *Who Wants a Cheap Rhinoceros?* Macmillan, 1964.

Zemach, Harve and Margot. *Awake and Dreaming.* Farrar, Straus &
Giroux, 1970.

Emotions, Senses and the Body

Aliki. *The Wish Workers.* Dial Press, 1962.

Barker, Eric J. and W. F. Millard, *The Five Senses.* Bowman Publishers,
1975

Berger, Terry. *I Have Feelings.* Behavioral Publications, 1971.

Brenner, Barbara. *Bodies.* E. P. Dutton, 1973.

Cohen, Miriam. *Best Friends.* Macmillan, 1971.

Ellison, Virginia *The Pooh Get-Well Book.* E. P. Dutton, 1973.

Ets, Marie Hall. *Talking Without Words.* Viking, 1968.

Fassler, Joan. *My Grandpa Died Today.* Behavioral Publications, 1971.

Freeman, Don. *Dandelion.* Viking, 1964.

Green, Mary McBurney. *Is It Hard? Is It Easy?* Young Scott, 1960.

Kantrowitz, Mildred. *I Wonder if Herbie's Home Yet.* Parents' Magazine Press, 1971.

Krasilovsky, Phyllis. *The Very Little Boy.* Doubleday, 1962.

———. *The Very Little Girl.* Doubleday, 1953.

———. *The Very Tall Little Girl.* Doubleday, 1969.

Krauss, Ruth. *This Thumbprint.* Harper & Row, 1967.

O'Neill, Mary. *Hailstones and Halibut Bones: Adventures in Color.*
Doubleday, 1961.

Rey, H. A. and M. *Curious George Goes to the Hospital.* Houghton
Mifflin, 1966.

Sever, J. A. *Johnny Goes to the Hospital.* Houghton Mifflin, 1953.

Simon, Mina and Howard. *If You Were an Eel, How Would You Feel?*
     Follett, 1963.
Udry, Janice May. *Let's Be Enemies.* Harper & Row, 1961.
Viorst, Judith. *Alexander and the Terrible, Horrible, No Good, Very
     Bad Day.* Atheneum, 1973.
_____. *I'll Fix Anthony.* Harper & Row, 1969.
Waber, Bernard. *Ira Sleeps Over.* Houghton Mifflin, 1972.
Zolotow, Charlotte. *The Hating Book.* Harper & Row, 1969.
_____. *William's Doll.* Harper & Row, 1972.

Everyday Life Events

Brown, Margaret Wise. *Goodnight Moon.* Harper & Row, 1947.
Brown, Myra. *First Night Away from Home.* Watts, 1960.
_____. *Pip Moves Away.* Golden Gate Junior Books, 1967.
Flack, Marjorie. *Angus Lost.* Doubleday, 1932.
Hoban, Russell. *A Bargain for Frances.* Harper & Row, 1970.
_____. *Bread and Jam for Frances.* Harper & Row, 1964.
Hoffman, Phyllis. *Steffie and Me.* Harper & Row, 1970.
Kantrowitz, Mildred. *Good-Bye Kitchen.* Parents' Magazine Press,
     1972.
Kellogg, Steven. *Can I Keep Him?* Dial Press, 1971.
Krauss, Ruth. *A Hole Is to Dig.* Harper & Row, 1952.
Lobel, Arnold. *Frog and Toad Together.* Harper & Row, 1972.
Mayer, Mercer. *There's a Nightmare in My Closet.* Dial Press, 1968.
Raskin, Ellen. *Nothing Ever Happens on My Block.* Atheneum, 1966.
Rockwell, Anne. *The Awful Mess.* Parents' Magazine Press, 1973.
Rosenbaum, Eileen. *Ronnie.* Parents' Magazine Press, 1969.

Family Relations

Aliki. *June 7!* Macmillan, 1972.
Borack, Barbara. *Grandpa.* Harper & Row, 1967.
Byars, Betsy. *Go and Hush the Baby.* Viking Press, 1971.
Hoban, Russell. *A Baby Sister for Frances.* Harper & Row, 1964.
Keats, Ezra Jack. *Peter's Chair.* Harper & Row, 1967.
Lionni, Leo. *Little Blue and Little Yellow.* Astor-Honor, 1959.

Occupations

Borack, Barbara. *Gooney.* Harper & Row, 1968.
Brown, Margaret Wise. *The Little Fireman.* Young Scott Books, 1952.
Freeman, Don. *Inspector Peckit.* Viking, 1972.
Gergely, Tibor. *Busy Day, Busy People.* Random House, 1973.
Kotzwinkle, William. *The Firemen.* Pantheon, 1969.
Lenski, Lois. *Policeman Small.* Walck, 1962.
Merriam, Eve, and Solbert, Ronni. *Mommies at Work.* Knopf, 1961.
―――. *Boys and Girls, Girls and Boys.* Holt, Rinehart & Winston, 1972.
Scarry, Richard. *What Do People Do All Day?* Random House, 1968.

Places

Bemelmans, Ludwig. *Madeline.* Viking, 1939.
Brown, Marcia. *Felice.* Scribner, 1958.
De Regniers, Beatrice Schenk. *Circus.* Viking, 1966.
Freeman, Don. *Corduroy.* Viking, 1970.
―――. *Norman the Doorman.* Viking, 1959.
―――. *Quiet! There's a Canary in the Library.* Golden Gate Junior Books, 1969.
Keith, Eros. *A Small Lot.* Bradbury Press, 1968.
Krasilovsky, Phyllis. *The Cow Who Fell in the Canal.* Doubleday, 1957.
Sauer, Julia. *Mike's House.* Viking, 1954.

Seasons

Chaffin, Lillie. *Bear Weather.* Macmillan, 1969.
Eicke, Edna. *What's Your Name.* Windmill Books, 1968.
Hopkins, Lee Bennett. *City Talk.* Knopf, 1970.
Howell, Ruth. *Everything Changes.* Atheneum, 1968.
Keats, Ezra Jack. *The Snowy Day.* Viking, 1962.
Kuskin, Karla. *In the Flaky Frosty Morning.* Harper & Row, 1969.
Lenski, Lois. *I Like Winter.* Walck, 1950.
―――. *Now It's Fall.* Walck, 1948.
Schick, Eleanor. *City in Summer.* Macmillan, 1969.
―――. *City in Winter.* Macmillan, 1970.
Sendak, Maurice. *Chicken Soup with Rice.* Harper & Row, 1962.

Sounds

Borten, Helen. *Do You Hear What I Hear?* Abelard-Schuman, 1960.
Branley, Franklyn M. *Flash, Crash, Rumble, and Roll.* Crowell, 1964.
_____. *High Sounds, Low Sounds.* Crowell, 1967.
Brown, Margaret Wise. *The City Noisy Book.* Harper, 1939.
_____. *The Country Noisy Book.* Harper, 1940.
_____. *The Indoor Noisy Book.* Harper, 1942.
_____. *The Seashore Noisy Book.* Harper, 1941.
_____. *Shhhhh . . . Bang.* Harper, 1943.
Elkin, Benjamin. *The Loudest Noise in the World.* Viking, 1954.
Flack, Marjorie. *Angus and the Ducks.* Doubleday, 1930.
Gaeddert, Lou Ann. *Noisy Nancy Norris.* Doubleday, 1965.
Gramatky, Hardie. *Little Toot.* G. P. Putnam, 1939.
Grifalconi, A. *City Rhythms.* Bobbs-Merrill, 1965.
Johnson, La Verne. *Night Noises.* Parents' Magazine Press, 1968.
Keats, Ezra Jack. *Whistle for Willie.* Viking, 1964.
McCloskey, Robert. *Lentil.* Viking, 1940.
McGovern, Ann. *Too Much Noise.* Houghton Mifflin, 1967.
Memling, Carl. *What's in the Dark?* Parents' Magazine Press, 1971.
Mosel, Arlene. *Tikki Tikki Tembo.* Holt, Rinehart & Winston, 1968.
Rand, Ann. *Listen! Listen!* Harcourt, Brace & World, 1970.

Transportation

Bate, Norman. *Who Built the Bridge?* Scribner, 1964.
_____. *Who Built the Highway?* Scribner, 1953.
Cameron, Polly. *The Green Machine.* Coward, McCann & Geoghegan, 1972.
D'Aulaire, Ingri and Edgar. *The Two Cars.* Doubleday, 1955.
Ets, Marie Hall. *Little Old Automobile.* Viking, 1948.
Lenski, Lois. *The Little Auto.* Walck, 1934.
_____. *The Little Fire Engine.* Walck, 1946.
_____. *The Little Sailboat.* Walck, 1937.
_____. *The Little Train.* Walck, 1973.
Piper, Watty. *The Little Engine That Could.* Platt & Munk, 1930.
Sandberg, Inger and Lasse. *The Boy with 100 Cars.* Delacorte, 1966.
Zaffo, George. *The Giant Nursery Book of Things That Go.* Doubleday, 1959. (Also published as *Airplanes and Trucks and Trains, Fire*

Engines, Boats and Ships and Building and Wrecking Machines.
Grosset & Dunlap, 1968.)

RECORDS

A very young child is fascinated by sounds. The tone of a mother's
voice, the drip of a faucet, the hum of a motor, the crashing of thunder,
the language of animals or people, intrigue him as he searches for their
sources and meanings. As he learns to recognize and then recreate
sounds himself, his tongue clackings become horses' hoofs, finger snap-
pings stand for complicated comments, screeches substitute for sirens.
Just as he learns to use words to communicate his thoughts, so does he
use sound effects to communicate to himself and others as he pretends
in play.

From sound to music is a short step. By combining sounds in different ways the child discovers rhythm, tempo, tone and pitch. A melody
may be created, and when words are added, a song is born. The fact
that nonsense words delight as much as those with meaning only serves
to underscore the power of sound itself. Indeed, the magic he finds in
poetry is heavily dependent on the appeal of the sounds of language.

As the child learns to coordinate the sounds from his environment
with the movement and thoughts available within himself, a world of
possibilities opens to him. He can move his fingers, hands, head, feet
and body with the sounds; he can add his voice and sing along with or
without music; he can find his ideas expressed through music; music
can give him new ideas to carry back to his private world. At this point
an extensive repertoire of songs and melodies can become a great asset
to a child. "I'll Race You Down the Mountain" may pop into his head
as he mounts his tricycle; chants like "Abiyoyo" or "Zulu Warrior" can
embellish a game of pirates or Indians. Lullabies can be used to sing
his babies to sleep, marches in the course of a parade, folk songs to
express his feelings and actions while playing. He can then add his own
words to a familiar tune, adapting it for a specific situation; make up
new tunes with old ones to guide him; and master more complicated
songs for the sheer fun of making them a part of himself.

The list of records that follows is in no way comprehensive. Rather,
a few albums that may illustrate different kinds of music children enjoy
and respond to are listed, keeping the above goals in mind: to acquaint
him with sounds, stimulate a variety of body responses, and furnish him

with a repertoire of songs which may both stimulate pretend play by their content and embellish it by being available when the child is involved in his own imagination. The myriad of stories available in recorded forms is ignored; so, too, are songs drawn from other lands. Two good sources for the latter are the Folkways Records series of folk songs and dances from many countries and the Hi Neighbor UNICEF series published by OMS Records. An appreciation of the great classics is also beyond our present scope, as are records that focus on teaching numbers or the alphabet. Finally, the following list is only a beginning. Almost anything by Ella Jenkins, Pete Seeger, Nancy Raven, Tom Glazer, Hap Palmer, Woodie Guthrie, Burl Ives or Alan Mills and others is destined to become treasured by a preschool child; only a few examples of their work appear here.

Abiyoyo. Pete Seeger (Folkways FT1500). The charming story of a giant monster who is tamed by a song about himself. The chant of "Abiyoyo" is particularly catching.

American Folk Songs for Children. Pete Seeger (Folkways FC7601). A collection of old favorites like "This Old Man," "She'll Be Comin' 'Round the Mountain" and "Train Is a-Coming," in a simple, direct style.

Authentic Sound Effects. Jack Holzman, creator and producer (Elektra Records EKS7251). Exactly what it sounds like, this record begins with the sound of a car skid, travels through the noises of many machines and life experiences, ends with the opening and closing of a squeaky door.

Background Music for Home Movies—Vol. 1 (Folkways FX6110). A variety of very short musical montages to fit moods and experiences from flying and frolicking to danger and pursuit. Excellent for expressing music through movement.

Birds, Beasts, Bugs and Little Fishes. Pete Seeger (Folkways FTS31504). A variety of simple chants and songs in many tempos and rhythms. One can easily envision children flapping their arms to "Fly Through My Window" and imitating animal sounds along with "I Had a Rooster."

Children's Songs. Johnny Richardson (Folkways FC7678). A charming conglomeration of songs and chants, from those with a strong story line ("Katy the Kangaroo") to the semi-nonsensical "Miss Polly."

Come On and Wake Up. Fred Rogers (Columbia CC24520)—songs

about the oldest toy, you are you, songs about anger, and pretending.

Dance Music for Pre-School Children (S & R Records 407). One side
features an extensive variety of rhythms; nursery rhymes with
musical variations on their original themes are on the other.

Dance, Sing and Listen Again—Vol. 2. Miss Nelson and Bruce (Dimen-
sion 5 D111). Of outstanding interest in this effective album is the
"Machines" sequence. Progressively more complex sounds represent technology as the child himself acts out the doings of a
machine.

Documentary Sounds, No. 1 (Folkways FX6181). This album from
Folkways' ingenious Sound Series contains sound effects likely to
be familiar to the young child. The major categories of sounds are
Human Sounds, Bells, Cars and Trucks, Construction, and Air-
craft.

Dogwood Soup. Shep Ginands (Pathways of Sound POS1023). Appealing folk songs, mostly for listening.

Free to Be You and Me. Marlo Thomas et al. (Bell 1110). Verbal
sketches and clever songs provide the child with opportunities to
improvise themes of modern life. The songs themselves are
rhythmic, infectious and useful, as a small child can be overheard
singing "And some kinds of help are the kinds of help we all can
do without" or "Mommies are people."

Getting to Know Myself. Hap Palmer (Activity Records AR543). A
good record with appealing rock beat for using music and body
expression together, as children smile, frown, stamp their feet or
laugh to "Feelings" or wiggle, shake, touch, rub, bend or turn to
"Turn Around." Directions are explicit.

It Could Be a Wonderful World (Motivation Records MR10). A fine
recording of popular American brotherhood songs.

It's Kiddie Time! (Topps L1584). Short stories which use music and
sound effects as illustrations. "The Magic Flying Song," complete
with sounds of airplanes, gunner-to-pilot dialogue, birds, bumble-
bees and Indians, is an example of the approach, as is "Around the
World on a Bubble" wherein traveling results in representative
music from Ireland, Italy, India, South America and the United
States.

Kindergarten Sing-Along, Album 2 (Classroom Materials CM1147).
An excellent collection of simple folk tunes from "Mr. Rabbit" to
"Cumbaya." Of special interest is "Hush-a-Bye," the verbal and
musical story of a mother's search for a lost lullaby.

Lullabies and Other Children's Songs with Nancy Raven (Pacific Cascade LPL7007–B). An extensive collection of very short songs and chants with a wide variety of sounds, rhythms and tempos.

"Me, Myself and I" (Young People's Records 11012). On one side are games with a variety of movements and rich make-believe content designed to be played on the blanket of a child's bed; on the other is "My Playful Scarf," music to be interpreted by pretending with scarves. Very directed.

Mod Marches. Hap Palmer (Activity Records AR527). This alternative to the classic marches of Sousa includes such contemporary gems as "Sergeant Pepper's Lonely Hearts Club Band." A collection of songs and chants that a child will eagerly make his own. It includes "The World of Wickum Wackum" and "Let's Build a Street."

Mother Goose and Nursery Rhymes. Many albums are easily available. Small children love the traditional nursery rhymes and games, whether spoken or sung, and use them spontaneously in a wide variety of solitary and social play situations.

Negro Folk Songs for Young People. Huddie Ledbetter (Leadbelly) (Folkways FC7533). Absorbing listening; a few appropriate for singing alone; all conducive to movement.

Peter and the Wolf. Prokofiev, narrated by Leonard Bernstein (Columbia CC25501). An excellent rendition of the timeless favorite; a reading of the story on the second side.

A Place of Your Own. Fred Rogers (Columbia CC24519)—songs about being lonely, finding quiet alone places like a corner, a step, under a table, songs about looking and listening.

Saturday Morning Children's Concert. Narrated by Dexter Michael (Golden Records LP219). Classical selections well described. The variety of themes and moods is impressive and useful for the child who can listen for several minutes.

Science Fiction Sound Effects Record. Mel Kaiser (Folkways FX6250). Exactly as named and fascinating.

Songs of Camp (Folkways FC7510). A children's chorus often joins in these renditions of old favorites, from "You Can't Get to Heaven" to "Sipping Cider Through a Straw."

Songs to Grow On. Woody Guthrie (Folkways FT1502), also known as *Songs to Grow On for Mother and Child: Nursery Days* (Folkways FC7675). Twelve of his classic chants sung as simply and honestly as he created them. These tunes form an excellent repertoire for bursting into spontaneous song during all sorts of everyday activities. *School Days* (Folkways FC7020). Especially good for preschoolers.

Won't You Be My Neighbor. Fred Rogers (Columbia CC34516). Songs about "Things I Don't Understand," about when a baby comes to your house, and about how you grow bigger. Other records by

Woody Guthrie's Children's Songs. Bob and Louise de Cormier (Golden Records LP238). Many of the master's classics, often jazzed up, including "Wild Aminul" and "Bling Blang."

You Are Special. Fred Rogers (Columbia CC24518)—several of his most well-known songs, written for and beloved by small children, including one that reassures children that they can't go down the drain!

You Read to Me, I'll Read to You. John Ciardi and his children (Spoken Arts SA835). Ciardi and his children read his poetry, often containing much humor. There are particularly marvelous sounds in "Arvin Marvin Lillisbee Fitch" and "What Night Would it Be?"

You'll Sing a Song and I'll Sing a Song. Ella Jenkins (Folkways FC7664). Chants and folk songs from the familiar to the novel. The title song is easily adapted to a situation, fitting in any words which seem appropriate.

A FEW SOURCES OF CHILDREN'S RECORDS

Bowmar Publications
622 Rodier Drive
Glendale, California 91201

Children's Music Center
5373 West Pico Boulevard
Los Angeles, California 90019

Children's Record Guild
27 Thompson Street
New York, New York 10012

Folkways/Scholastic Records
906 Sylvan Avenue
Englewood Cliffs, New Jersey 07632

Adult Reading List

Aronoff, Frances Webber. *Music and Young Children.* Holt, Rinehart & Winston, 1969. An excellent technical book on the structure and content of music and ways in which they may be applied to teaching music to young children.

Bonny, Helen L., and Savary, Louis M. *Music and Your Mind.* Harper & Row, 1973. A book describing techniques to develop imagination by relating music to the imaginative process.

Cherry, Clare. *Creative Movement for the Developing Child.* Rev. ed. Fearon Publishers (Lear Siegler, Inc., Educational Division, Belmont, Cal.), 1968. An approach to teaching movement and some games that have worked for at least one nursery school teacher.

Croft, Doreen J., and Hess, Robert D. *An Activities Handbook for Teachers of Young Children.* Houghton Mifflin, 1972. Excellent sections and activities relating to music and movements. Good bibliographies.

Nash, Grace E. *Music with Children: Verses and Movement, Primary to Upper Levels.* Kitching Educational (Le Grange, Ill.), 1967. Extensive collection of songs and games for children.

Ring a Ring of Roses. Flint Public Library (Flint, Mich.), 1971. Detailed descriptions of dozens of finger games and acting-out songs for preschool children.

Sheehy, Emma D. *Children Discover Music and Dance.* Teachers College Press (New York), 1968. Multidimensional approach to music

and movement from reasons why to ways to. Bibliographies of
songbooks, books about dance, records.

Stecher, Miriam. "Concept Learning Thru Movement Improvisation:
The Teacher's Role as Catalyst," in *Ideas That Work with Young
Children,* pp. 112–122. National Association for the Education of
Young Children (Washington, D.C.), 1972. Concrete ways in
which a teacher can be flexible and spontaneous and still teach.

Research Bibliography

Action for Children's Television. 46 Austin Street, Newtonville, Mass. 02160.

Beckwith, J. "People at Play: We Build Our Own Playground." Paper presented at Second Annual Symposium on Play at Georgia State University, April 1974.

Children's Advertising Guidelines. Children's Review Unit, National Advertising Division, Council of Better Business Bureaus, 845 Third Avenue, New York, N.Y. 10022.

Dattner, R. *Design for Play.* Van Nostrand Reinhold, 1969.

DeMille, Richard. *Put Your Mother on the Ceiling: Children's Imagination Games.* Viking, 1973.

Educational Arts Association, 90 Sherman Street, Cambridge, Mass. 02140

Erikson, Erik. *Childhood and Society.* Norton, 1963.

Far West Laboratory for Educational Research and Development. In Reinhold, R. "Lending Libraries for Educational Toys." *The New York Times,* May 4, 1975.

Fein, Greta. "A Transformational Analysis of Pretending." *Developmental Psychology* II (1975), 291–296.

Fein, G., and Robertson, A. "Cognitive and Social Dimensions of Two-Year-Olds." Mimeographed report, Yale University, 1974.

Fineman, J. "Observations on the Development of Imaginative Play in Early Childhood." *Journal of the American Academy of Child Psychiatry* I (1962), 167–181.

Freyberg, J. "Increasing the Imaginative Play of Urban Disadvantaged Kindergarten Children Through Systematic Training." Chapter in J. L. Singer, *The Child's World of Make-Believe*. Academic Press, 1973.

Gesell, Arnold, Frances L. Ilg, Louise Bates Ames, and Janet Learned Rodell. *Infant and Child in the Culture of Today*. Rev. ed. Harper & Row, 1974.

Giambra, L. "Daydreaming Across the Life Span: Late Adolescent to Senior Citizen." *International Journal of Aging and Human Development* 5 (1974), 116–135.

Gould, R. *Child Studies Through Fantasy*. Quadrangle Books, 1972.

Herron, R. E., and Sutton-Smith, B., eds. *Child's Play*. Wiley, 1971.

Hill, P. *Creative Playground*. Children's Environments Advisory Service Central Mortgage and Housing Corporation Head Office. Ottawa, Canada KIA OP7.

Kelly, E. *The Magic If.* Drama Book Specialists (New York), 1973.

Levenstein, P. Parent-Training Program. Cited in Kenner, L. "Toys and Disadvantaged Children." *The New York Times*, May 26, 1973.

Lewin, K. *A Dynamic Theory of Personality*. McGraw-Hill, 1935.

Liebert, R. *The Early Window: Effects of Television on Children and Youth*. Pergamon Press, 1973.

Piaget, J. *The Language and Thought of the Child*. Harcourt, Brace, 1932.

———— *Play, Dreams and Imitation in Childhood*. Norton, 1962.

Piaget, J., and Inhelder, B. *Mental Imagery in the Child*. Basic Books, 1971.

Play Laboratory for Multiply Handicapped Children, University of Massachusetts. Amherst, Mass. 01003.

Pulaski, M. "Toys and Imaginative Play." Chapter in J. L. Singer, *The Child's World of Make-Believe*. Academic Press, 1973.

Saltz, E. *Training for Thematic Play in Culturally-Disadvantaged Children*. Annual report to Spencer Foundation. Center for Cognitive Studies, Wayne State University, Detroit, Mich., 1976.

Singer, J. L. *The Child's World of Make-Believe: Experimental Studies of Imaginative Play*. Academic Press, 1973.

————. *The Inner World of Daydreaming*. Harper & Row, 1975.

Singer, J. L., and Singer, D. G. "Imaginative Play and Pretending in Early Childhood." In A. Davids, ed. *Child Personality and Psychopathology*. Vol. 3. Wiley, 1976.

————. "TV—A Member of the Family." *Yale Alumni Magazine* xxxviii, no. 6. (1975), 10–15.

Smilansky, S. *The Effects of Sociodramatic Play on Disadvantaged Pre-school Children.* Wiley, 1968.

Stewart, Kilton. "Dream Theory in Malaya." Chapter in Charles Tart, editor, *Altered States of Consciousness.* Wiley, 1969.

Stone, L. J., and Church, J. *Childhood and Adolescence.* 3rd ed. Random House, 1973.

Index